PRAISE FOR *MONEY, LOVE & LEGACY*

"How little we understand about money and love and how they work together, but all too often against each other. Helga Hayse helps us understand much that we ought to know... about the ways for us to begin needed conversations across the generation chasm, and the divide that follows all too often from pain, hurt and misunderstandings. She has managed a distillation in Money Love & Legacy of poignant and revealing narratives, including her own compelling story, with guidance that is practical, sound and ultimately resonant with hope."

— *Michael Krasny, host of KQED Forum and author of Off Mike: A Memoir of Talk Radio and Literary Life*

"A common sense approach to rethinking personal relationships in the light of not-so-intuitively obvious cognitive science discoveries. Makes you question many of your most cherished beliefs about yourself and others."

— *Robert Burton, MD, author of On Being Certain: Believing That You Are Right Even When You're Not*

"As a former ER physician, I've seen families arrive too late for the conversations presented in this book. In my current role as chaplain for spiritual care, I've seen the peace that comes to families who can have these conversations. Helga Hayse provides a gentle and clear guide to the territory most of us avoid – the conversations of the heart. Physicians, nurses, social workers and anyone who guides families towards open, loving and clear communication can gain tremendously from reading this book."

— *Bruce Feldstein, MD, Director, The Jewish Chaplaincy at Stanford University Medical Center*

"A pathway, guide and instruction book for dealing with two taboo subjects – money and death. Helga shows how families can avoid misunderstandings about these two issues. This book should be mandatory reading for every parent and adult child. It will bring clarity and closure, while teaching all how to manage and deal with money, love and legacy."

— *Stan Jernigan*
Founder, The Mentor Group

Money, Love & Legacy

Conversations That Matter
Between Generations

Helga Hayse

ISBN 0977836835   Print Edition
Library of Congress Control Number: 2010900919
Primelife Publishing
San Mateo, California 94402

PUBLISHER'S NOTE

The individual experiences recounted in this book are true. However, in some instances, names and descriptive details have been changed to protect the privacy of the people involved.

This publication is intended to provide general guidelines. Readers are urged to seek qualified professional legal and financial information before taking any steps for formal estate planning, financial planning or medical procedures.

Printed in the United States of America
Design by Lee Saunders Wright

Dedication

For my parents who knew not what they did,
Yet gave me life and my own chance.

Prologue

Give Them the Flowers Now

Closed eyes can't see the white roses;
Cold hands can't hold them, you know.
Breath that is stilled cannot gather
The odors that sweet from them blow.
Death, with a peace beyond dreaming
Its children of earth doth endow;
Life is the time we can help them;
So give them the flowers now.

Here are the struggles and striving;
Here are the cares and the tears;
Now is the time to be smoothing
The frowns and the furrows and fears.
What, to closed ears, are kind sayings?
What, to hushed heart, is deep vow?
Naught can avail after parting,
So give them the flowers now.

Anonymous

Contents

Contents

Introduction

W hat if today was your last chance to speak to the people you love, your last opportunity to share what's in your heart and your mind?

The cell phone buzzed in Colin's pocket; a text from Jan, his sister. "Dad's in the hospital. Heart attack. Operation tomorrow." The son excused himself from the weekly staff meeting, asked his assistant to book a flight to Manhattan, and hailed a cab for LAX. He called his wife to let her know where he was going, and called his mother to tell her he was on his way.

Colin feared that he might not get there in time - to say things he'd wanted to say to his father for a long time, but it never seemed like the right time. He wanted to tell him how much he admired, respected and loved him; how grateful he was to have him as a father, how he appreciated the sacrifices and support, and how much he learned from him. As he looked out the airplane window, Colin realized he might never be able to talk with his father again.

At the hospital in Manhattan, his father Frank was conscious and stabilized, but frightened and hooked up to life saving equipment in the ICU. His wife Anne told him the kids were on their way; they'd be here before the surgery in the morning. Frank hoped he'd have the strength and courage to say what he'd wanted to say to his children for so long, but it somehow had never been the right time. He'd wanted to share the details of his estate plan. He'd wanted to tell them how proud he was of them, what fine people they'd turned out to be after all the problem years of adolescence, about his regrets for the things he didn't do for *and with* them as a father. Frank wasn't a religious man but he so desperately wanted to give Colin and Jan his blessing. He closed his eyes and hoped that they would arrive before his surgery.

This scenario happens in some form or other countless times a day. A parent or child realizes that the things each wanted to say to the other may never be said. They think they have all the time in the world for what they know are crucial conversations, but they're wrong. Like Colin and his family, they may only have today.

Whether it's a talk about money, the expression and actions of love or the legacy with which a parent will be remembered, if they fail to initiate the important conversations from the heart, they miss out on the chance to clear up misunderstandings, forgive wrongs and resolve unfinished business. Too often, when a parent dies, children are burdened with feelings of anger, guilt, shame, doubt, abandonment and regret about a relationship that is central to their life. These feelings, often unconscious, infrequently articulated, interfere with their ability to move 'cleanly' through their grief. Having the conversations before it's too late can spare them these negative emotions.

My friend Marcia took a bold step in that direction by writing the following letter to her father when his struggle against lung cancer took a turn for the worse.

> Dear Daddy,
>
> Although we both dance around the subject, we never really say to each other what we both know – that you are approaching the end of your inspiring, heroic, joyful and worthy life. Before we say goodbye and you leave me, I want to tell you how you shaped me into the woman I am today. From my earliest memories, you inspired me and taught me that I could do anything. You nourished my dreams and supported my goals by your faith in me. Thank you for the gifts of your love, acceptance and belief. You will live for me always and I will love you until my own last breath.   Marcia

I never got the chance to say to my father what Marcia managed to say to hers before he died. I didn't even get the chance to say goodbye. A decision I made - to marry outside of our faith- had unexpected repercussions and split us apart. If I had known then what I know now, and what I share with you in this book, I might have been able to heal our wounds and tell him of my love. My parents died over two decades ago, and the grief I carry with me is still profound. In contrast, when my husband died, I grieved far more cleanly. By pure good luck, we had had the chance to say what we needed to say to each other. We had no unfinished business, and that allowed me to heal with 'clean grief.'

I wrote this book with the understanding of how difficult it can be to start these conversations. I provide guidelines for you in a variety of areas – the practical, the emotional and the spiritual. I share my own experiences of having, and not having, crucial conversations with my family. You will read about people who were kind enough to share their thoughts, fears and concerns with me about unfinished business within their own families. I've changed their names and identifying details to protect their privacy.

I offer you some food for thought, some inconvenient truths and some guidelines for carrying on crucial conversations about issues of money, love and legacy between you, your parents and your adult children. Together, I hope they provide navigation tools for intergenerational dialogue, appreciation and blessing, and where necessary, forgiveness.

Hundreds of books can give you the details of estate and financial planning. I wrote this one to provide a different framework for thinking about relationships between generations. Parents and children don't like to think that money and love have any relationship to each other. Unfortunately, this is a myth; money insinuates itself into family relationships, whether we like to admit it or not.

Under the best of circumstances, money is a touchy

and often difficult subject to raise. In the context of discussing inheritance or financial planning, the resistance increases and the discomfort is magnified tenfold. The word 'legacy' is often used by the financial planning community interchangeably with inheritance. In fact, legacy is something which parents create as they raise their children, and for which they will be remembered by their family and the community. It is not the same thing as inheritance at all. No - money, love, and legacy are three separate areas. It is important that we tease them apart as we open up crucial conversations with the people we love.

In the process of researching and writing this book, I was surprised and affected by insights I didn't anticipate. For example, I learned that we all have our illusions about the kind of person we are and how that impacts our relationship to our parents or children. My friend Nancy, who lived in Italy for many years, admitted how resentful she felt when she returned to the United States to help her mother after her father died. Nancy had never been close to her mother. Living and working abroad as a journalist allowed Nancy to think of herself as a good daughter who lived far away because she had to, not because she wanted to. When her mother asked for her help, Nancy had to address her relationship issues with her mother, which she could ignore while living overseas.

Mary told me how she tried to sabotage her father's relationship with a new woman a few years after he was widowed. Mary claimed that the woman was a gold digger and only cared about her father's money. Her real reason was her concern that her inheritance would be affected if part of her father's estate went to his new wife. She said she knew it wasn't right, but believed she and her children should get it all.

My research also showed me that whatever we're certain about, it's often not true, even when we're certain that it is. In chapter six, called The Dangers of Certainty, I'll go into detail about the ways in which we assure ourselves that we're right, and justify what we believe.

Perhaps most important, I learned that it's not just what we say that matters, but what we don't say, that lives on to trouble us when it's no longer possible to speak. Just as Colin and his father failed to say important things to each other, because they "could never find the right moment," each of us could find ourself in a similar 'racing-to-the-bedside' scenario. Colin's father made it through surgery, and father and son did have the chance to share their conversations from the heart. But it could just as easily have gone the other way. Colin would have carried regrets for the rest of his life about what he didn't get the chance to say to his father.

That's why I want you to move past the resistance that keeps you from opening the crucial conversations with your parents or your children. They're crucial because they deal with memories of times you were in pain, regrets you may not realize you have and amends you may want to make. Clearing them will protect you, your parents and your children from having to bear an additional, unnecessary and painful burden if any of you should die.

The details will vary in every family story, but the common thread is the same: something happened, it wasn't understood, discussed, or forgiven. It can change the foundation of the family relationship from then on – unless you learn to untangle what's really happening. That's what I'm hoping you'll learn from this book.

I was widowed when my husband died in an accident. For months I couldn't sleep or think clearly. I felt numb, weepy, unable to eat, restless. Yet I noticed a curious thing. Unlike so many widows I meet through my work, I didn't feel any guilt or anger toward my husband. My grief was 'clean,' not muddied by an accumulation of things I had wanted to say to him. Having those crucial conversations didn't just happen. We procrastinated, using every excuse we could think of; our schedules were full, we barely had time for our friends and family, it wasn't our favorite thing to do and dozens more.

Finally, I asked my husband to try an exercise with me, that I was planning to introduce into the workshops I presented for women about finances and marriage. To him, this didn't feel like a 'conversation about the relationship,' but a concrete way to help me improve my workshops. The engineer in him wasn't going to pass up an opportunity to streamline something or make it work more efficiently. He agreed to have this conversation from the heart with me based on a series of questions I wrote for the workshop.

Had my husband lived, the results of our honesty and openness would have influenced the quality of our marriage. When he died, I realized the full value of what we had done. I share the questions we explored in the last part of this book.

Whereas the wound from my husband's death healed in time like a clean surgical incision, my parents' death left me with emotional scar tissue which took years to heal. It's no mystery why that is so. My husband and I had our crucial conversations; my parents and I did not. If we had, I am certain that their deaths would not have haunted me for so long.

When you finish this book, you will understand why we confuse and equate money and love. You'll get a deeper look at what you really want from your parents and children. You'll realize who benefits the most from forgiveness. And you will know how to avoid the 'if only' syndrome.

Perhaps most important, you will know how to resolve the 'unfinished business' with the people you love, so that you don't carry the burden of regret after they are gone.

As the poet Rainier Maria Rilke wrote, "live the questions now. Perhaps then, someday far in the future, you will gradually live your way into the answer."

1 What, Me Worry?

How Facing Mortality Strengthens Our Life

> "I'm not afraid to die.
> I just don't want to be there when it happens."
>
> Woody Allen

Shakespeare called death "the undiscovered country," a universal experience for which we have no guidelines. Nothing we do in life can protect us from it. Death is the one experience we will all share. Planning a legacy means putting the fact of our death squarely in the center and looking at the interconnecting threads of our life. Who wants to even think about it?

So we don't. We find all kinds of ways around the subject: we deny, we procrastinate, we excuse, we're superstitious. Some of us whistle, cheerfully optimistic or reverentially prayerful, hoping that our prayers will be answered. None of these behaviors hurt us; they hurt the ones we love.

Comedian Alan King had a nightclub routine that involved reading obituaries about men who are survived by their wives. The obituaries were sent to him by fans to support King's assertion that wives outlive their husbands. King invited audience members to read out loud from the obituaries, each of which was more bizarre than the previous one. The hilarity mounted as King repeated the last line "SURVIVED BY HIS WIFE." The routine brought down the house every time.

It's easy to laugh at jokes about death. Perhaps we do that because humor is a way of dealing with pain, fear and the unknown. We stop laughing however, when the subject hits too close to home.

As a culture, Americans avoid talking about death. We have euphemisms for dying. People 'pass away' or 'cross over.' But our awareness of mortality is always with us individually, barely audible, just under the veil of consciousness.

Writing a will, planning an inheritance and thinking about a legacy means pulling aside that veil and confronting the certain fact that we *will* die. Most of us have spent a lifetime suppressing this knowledge through a variety of distractions: denial, superstition, procrastination, prayer, hope, optimism, alcohol, drugs, to name just a few. None of them stop the clock or change the final outcome.

Who wants to think about that? Not us, not our kids, not our parents. Whether it's facing our own death, or the loss of a parent or child, we'd rather be thinking about almost anything else.

The newspaper industry did a study years ago about which pages readers turned to first. The results showed that the first was the sports section, the second, the obituaries. Why? Reading or hearing about the tragedy or death of other people gives us a temporary reprieve. In a perverse sort of way, it feels comforting; if we're reading about others, it means we're still here.

We're reminded periodically of our mortality through news about natural disasters, airplane crashes, celebrity deaths and lumps in breasts. Such painful reminders rivet our attention on our fragility. When Princess Diana died, millions of strangers mourned her death - not so much out of sympathy for her, but rather from the traumatic collective realization that even the most privileged can meet with unexpected tragedy.

For the same reason, we cannot comfortably watch interviews with the paralyzed, wheelchair-bound Stephen Hawking, a brilliant astronomer whose mind is still sharp, but whose ability to speak and move has been felled by Lou Gehrig's disease. We are disturbed to see Michael J. Fox struggle to maintain his equilibrium as his Parkinson's disease progresses. As brave as Christopher Reeves was after his fall from a horse, the Superman of cinema disturbingly reminded us of our own frailty and powerlessness.

As a nation, we're stunned when a Michael Jackson dies, seemingly in good health. When Farrah Fawcett died, we watched through our own repressed anxiety as she fought against cancer, tracking down every possible cure in her effort to stay alive. People in the public eye are people we identify with, yet at the same time, we distance ourselves from them. Yes, death and tragedy happen to others. That doesn't mean they will happen to us. But they will – we just don't know when.

Fear of Planning is Fear of Death

There are two dimensions to the concept of death; the death of another and the death of one's self. When someone else dies, it's an event that happens within the world where we live. Even if the death is of a person we love, we experience the anguish of loss in our world, the world we know. We grieve the loss in an environment of familiar things. Our pain is proof that we are still here, still alive.

In contrast, when we imagine our own death, we are confronted with the disappearance of our self, the end of the world as we know it. We have the stories we've been taught about what happens after death. Heaven and hell are real concepts for believers who often spend a lifetime worrying about whether they will make it to heaven. For those who don't embrace these concepts, there is the void, the fear of no thing. This is terrifying to think about – and so, we don't.

Psychiatrists have long equated the reluctance to think about drawing up a will or an estate plan with the fear of death. Writing a will means having to admit our mortality. It means thinking about giving up our possessions and power. Perhaps most important, it means asking ourselves difficult questions about our relationships with our family.

Say the word "widow" to many men and you go straight to the heart of their own fears about death. The phrase 'planning for your loved ones,' can set in motion a chain of emotional reactions that results in wiping out a person's illusion of immortality.

But we're wrong to hide from death. Recognizing what facing death can do for us and for the people we love is a mature act of wisdom. In fact, if we don't do it, we're turning our back on one of the most important parts of our life – who we are and how we want to be remembered.

For we will be remembered, and not always as we'd like to be. Death focuses the mind…and that's the problem.

Even believers in an immortal soul, an afterlife and eternity, harbor secret fears about death. What if none of it is true? What if everything is myth - fairy tales to comfort us in the absence of real information?

Irvin Yalom, psychiatrist and author, writes in his latest book *Staring at the Sun: Overcoming the Terror of Death*, that death anxiety, hidden and disguised, is the wellspring of many of our worries, stresses, and conflicts. Yalom counsels terminal patients who are facing the near-term prospect of their death. He also sees physically healthy patients who suffer from ontological anxiety, the ever present terror of non-being, that isn't dispelled by Prozac or Valium.

Yalom describes his personal journey of making peace with his own death by calling on the wisdom of ancient philosophers. He singles out Epicurus, his personal favorite, as a man without illusions who believed in enjoying the moment, because death is the end of sense experience. We know Epicurus as the source of the word *epicure* or *epicurean*, signifying a person devoted to refined sensuous enjoyment (especially good food and drink). Epicurus believed that the root cause of misery is our omnipresent fear of death, that interferes with our enjoyment of life.

Yalom introduces the concept of *rippling*, which he describes as "leaving behind something from our life experience; some trait; some piece of wisdom, guidance, virtue, comfort that passes on to others, known and unknown." Think of tossing a stone into a pool of water. The water creates ripples that extend in a widening circle. Yalom suggests that each of us exists in "concentric circles of influence" that affect people, even if the person who created the ripple never receives acclaim or acknowledgement.

I often experience rippling in my life. For example,

on a flight that was finally ready to depart after a three hour delay for repairs, one of the passengers was missing. The additional delay to search for the wayward flyer left many of the 300 passengers even more irritated and surly. The purser kept her calm, and assured us that takeoff would be within minutes. While the flight was airborne, I talked with the purser about the stresses of her job. I'll never forget the wisdom she shared.

"I've been with the airline for 18 years," she said. "I fly 12 days out of 30. I love my job, the pay is good and my family is healthy. The rest is entertainment."

I had never thought about it that way before. If I were faced with hundreds of grumbling, jet-lagged people demanding information and telling me how rotten my employer is, I don't know if I would have kept my cool the way she did.

Think of it... *the rest is entertainment*. What a marvelous tool she shared with me for how she separates temporary irritations from the things that really matter in her life. She may not remember me, or the brief exchange we shared, but I will never forget it. Her words struck me as being so wise, and having such clarity, that I've repeated her story countless times.

In other words, the wisdom she shared *rippled* through me to many other people. They now have a tool to help them distinguish between the transitory and the truly important areas of their own life. It's a small thing perhaps, but so much about how we are remembered is based on small things.

The effects of rippling surround us. The influence of authors, artists, teachers, musicians and philanthropists are obvious examples. Most of us won't get the chance to endow a university chair or get our name on a building, but there are dozens of ways in which we influence people; the friendly smile, the helping hand, the unexpected gift. What will survive us are the human connections we make, the ways in which we touch other lives in secret and untold ways. The wisdom and guidance we share and the kindness and comfort we pass on to others - the ripples - known or unknown.

Distractions to Crucial Conversations

Denial

One of the most common reasons people don't plan for death is denial. Denial is the mechanism that allows us to censor ourselves before thoughts or feelings can surface. Even ostriches can be smarter than we are.

The ostrich. Ever stand close to one? Some of them are nearly seven feet tall. Soft feathers can be died any color to make great accessories. And check out those eyes, hooded lids ringed with lashes which flutter languidly while looking right past you.

But inside that head is a brain smaller than its eye. Perhaps that's why the ostrich, when it senses danger, lays its neck flat on the ground or buries its head in the sand, and thinks it can't be seen. It's laughable – the ostrich believes it's safe because "if I can't see you, you can't see me."

In many ways, we humans behave like the ostrich. We may try to justify our behavior with reasonable explanations and noble intentions, but we're still sticking our heads in the sand. In fact, this tendency is so like the behavior of the giant bird that it's named for it: the *Ostrich Syndrome*. This syndrome is evidenced when we behave in ways we convince ourselves are safe, when in reality, they represent wishful thinking on our part. We refuse to think logically about them. Or we hope nothing bad will happen. Or we think the odds are in our favor. Or we pray and believe our prayers will be answered. Or we think a positive mental attitude will protect us against the things we can't control. We learn the tactics of self-deception very early. In fact, we need those protective fictions to survive. Daniel Goleman writes in *Vital Lies, Simple Truths: The Psychology of Self-Deception* that "our blind spots and protective fictions allow us to live our lives and have our relationships function, sometimes smoothly, sometimes not. We all have blind spots, individually and culturally, balancing what is lacking and closing that gap by what we create."

Do we really see what we look at? The best evidence suggests not; we see what we look *for*. We don't notice what is irrelevant until something makes it relevant. We believe we won't age, that our children will always love us, our spouse will be faithful and that we won't die until we're ready. Reality intrudes when wrinkles deepen, children renounce us, a spouse becomes secretive about credit card charges or we receive a diagnosis of a serious illness.

Protective fictions are self-created blind spots, things we think about that we don't want to know we're thinking. These protective fictions or narratives that we tell ourselves (and others) help us to avoid acknowledging that the large shadow in the living room must belong to something.

Blind spots are useful for getting some of our relationship needs met; an agreement not to press for those that aren't being addressed. It's a Faustian bargain, whether made consciously or unconsciously: "I won't bring this up if you don't bring that up." The price for this silence, however, is costly, and ultimately self-defeating.

The Upside of Denial

Denial is the emotional drug-of-choice for so many of us. Oddly enough, the ostrich is not in denial when it feels in danger. Remember that small brain? It thinks it is taking action to protect itself by burying its head in the sand. "I don't see you; therefore, you can't see me" is not denial. It's lack of reasoning ability.

The amazing thing about denial is that when we're in it, we don't know it. The world seems to be as it appears. Just as fish don't know they swim in water until someone pulls the plug in the aquarium, we don't know we're in denial about death until we or someone we love is presented with a life threatening event or condition. That's when our awareness of vulnerability hits home.

We refuse to believe that, when it comes to longevity, we are not in control of the outcome. Destiny is a numbers game, an impersonal statistic. Prepared or not, the odds are the same; something either will happen or it won't. Cancer happens. Accidents occur. Planes crash. We lose people we love. Superstition does not help. Prayer does not help. Logic does not help. Most of the time, we have no control.

Religion tries to eliminate even the whiff of coincidence. When good things happen, we like to think God had a hand in it, especially if we've prayed for it. When hoping that a bad thing won't happen, we leverage all the tools at our disposal – superstition, denial, prayer, hope, or those good old reliable protective fictions.

A random universe is frightening; it makes us feel ordinary and vulnerable. Realizing that things 'just happen' means accepting randomness. We want events to logically 'belong' somewhere. Thinking that we are part of a grand plan gives us the illusion of leverage and control. But as John Lennon wrote in his song "Beautiful Boy," "Life is what happens while you're busy making other plans."

We also don't recognize which things are in our control. Ironically, one of the things we can control is planning for the things we can't. A few years ago I went on safari in Kenya. When we visited the Masai Mara, we noticed that the young Masai women had a gap in their lower front teeth. Apparently, lockjaw was a recurring problem. By knocking out their front teeth, women of childbearing age could still nurse their babies even if they contracted tetanus, because they could drink their nourishing beverage of milk and blood. Since tetanus shots to protect against lockjaw are not generally available in the Masai Mara, this is good planning.

Denial is the refusal to accept things as they are. It can be a powerful antidote to anxiety, but does little to change the source of that anxiety. Mardi Horowitz, a psychiatrist, writes in her book *The Denial of Stress* that there are many forms of denial, stating that "we realign the facts to obscure what is really going on. It's useful because we repress what we fear. The world seems normal and we're not particularly bothered by what we don't know."

We don't want to be reminded of our mortality. But if you are a parent, it's selfish not to face it, because your denial will leave your children unprotected. If you are an adult child whose parents refuse to talk with you about end-of-life care (or inheritance, legacy, medical preferences and other subjects that will impact you if they become ill), you will not be able to help them when something happens

We treat death with an awe and respect that ought to be reserved for life. Acknowledging our vulnerability to events beyond our control increases our appreciation of the preciousness of daily life. Perhaps, being able to discuss death with someone we care about is a form of intimacy; we have no reason to discuss it with someone who isn't important in our life. Whether it's our spouse, our parents or our children, the fact that we love them enough to trust them with our feelings about one of our deepest fears is a profound act of love.

Education about death is education about life. Lily Pincus writes in *Death and the Family*: "Thinking and talking about death need not be morbid. It may be quite the opposite. Ignorance and fear of death overshadow life, while knowing about and accepting death erases this shadow and makes life freer of fears and anxieties."

I bought a grave so my children won't be faced with confusion about my burial wishes. I showed them where it is, not far from where my home is. We joked about how nice the view is and that the tree near my piece of real estate is great for leaning against if they come to visit. Keeping it light means keeping it in perspective. It serves as an example for them, too, in how to discuss death with their own children.

Superstition

When my mother heard bad news, she would rush for the salt shaker, turn on the gas stove and sprinkle salt for 30 seconds into the flame, certain that with this gesture she was protecting herself against something bad happening to her family.

Superstitions like this are harmless: knocking on wood, carrying a rabbit's foot, hoping that if you get on a plane with your right foot that the plane won't crash. I do this last one myself. Silly and harmless. But some superstitions are not so innocuous.

For example, the notion that talking about some-

19

thing will cause it to occur makes many people super-stitious about estate planning.

Ed and Cynthia have been married for 35 years. This is his second marriage. He's been a good husband and he loves her dearly. But Ed has this quirk – he believes that if he signs the durable powers of attorney paper-work as part of their estate plan, God, who is always watching, will decide it's time for Ed to die.

Because Ed won't sign the necessary papers, Cynthia won't be able to act on his behalf if he can't make med-ical or financial decisions for himself. His adult children from his first marriage will have the power to do that.

"Ed signed the other estate planning documents, but won't sign the durable powers of attorney," she said. "He says he will, but when I remind him that the plan-ning isn't complete unless he does sign, he accuses me of nagging. He knows not signing isn't rational, but he says it makes him feel better. Even though I understand his thinking, I feel like a hostage to his superstition."

Is there any difference between that kind of thinking and not walking under a ladder, wearing garlic around your neck to protect yourself from vampires or crossing the street when you see a black cat?

I discovered in interviews that many men left loose ends in their estate planning and procrastinated about completing the process. It wasn't laziness, but *fear* that was responsible for this lack of action.

For example, William just kept 'forgetting' to fill out the papers to fund the revocable trust he and his wife Lila had set up. Their lawyer explained that, until their financial assets were transferred into the trust, the trust wasn't considered a legal entity. That meant that if something happened to William, the trust couldn't pro-vide Lila with the legal or financial protection for which it was originally intended.

When I spoke with William, he said he'd been busy, had other things on his mind and just never got around to it, but he would make the transfers as soon as he had a minute. Yes, the lawyer had offered to take care of it, but he preferred to do it himself.

Meanwhile, Lila's hands are tied because William doesn't want her to take care of it either. "My husband's friend had a fatal heart attack on the tennis court the day after he and his wife signed their living trust," she said. "You try convincing my husband that the same won't happen to him."

Superstition is a powerful, if irrational and usually subconscious, belief that keeps many people from taking action to protect their family in case they die. It presumes a causal relationship between something we do (or don't do) and the outcome of some future event. It's comforting to think that a higher power is watching over us, waiting until all the papers are in order and everything is signed before taking us away. For example, my husband died 30 days after our estate plan documents were signed. Was there any connection between the signing and his death?

Of course not. Believing we're at the center of the universe in this way is another example of wishful thinking. Unfortunately, tragic events don't wait to occur until we're prepared for them. So, when people won't follow through with the necessary arrangements to protect their family, superstition can have a devastating impact.

Legal and financial consequences operate in the real world. Good intentions don't count; drafts of legal documents don't count. If you're not protected by signed and witnessed estate plan documents, none of the planning you do counts.

Procrastination

Psychologists know there are many complex, powerful and not always obvious reasons we procrastinate. They include issues around helplessness, fear of failure, self-esteem, independence and dependence and a host of others. The *reasons* we have these feelings are not addressed by procrastination, but the feelings themselves are avoided for awhile.

Most of us assume that we procrastinate because we lack willpower. The opposite is true: when we procrastinate, we're actually demonstrating a lot of willpower - *for certain things*. We're very good at deciding what we will pay attention to.

Procrastination is essentially dealing with a challenge by avoiding it. But the avoidance isn't just connected to completing a project. For example, William, whom we met earlier, 'conveniently' forgets to finish the paperwork that would make his estate plan complete. But he never procrastinates about completing the sailboat he's building. He looks forward to the fun he'll have exploring local waterways. In other words, his feelings about what he wants to do *match* his willingness to do it. But he wants to avoid the feelings he gets when he thinks about what completing the estate plan means.

I watched a tragic combination of procrastination and optimism play out in the life of Donna and Ted. They own and run a sheep ranch 15 miles outside of Omaha. The ranch is connected to the main road by a rickety bridge spanning a narrow river. One evening, as a storm approached, Ted realized he still had business to attend to in town. He knew Donna was concerned about the bridge, so he reassured her he'd be back before the storm hit.

The storm hit early; the bridge held. But Ted's heart didn't. By the time Donna made it to the hospital, Ted was hooked up to life support. His eyes were closed; he couldn't talk. Ted's sons consulted with the doctor, but they ignored Donna. Even after ten years, the boys still resented their father's remarriage after their mother died.

Feeling invisible and helpless, Donna began to sob. If her husband survived, he would need heart surgery and extensive rehabilitation. His outdated estate plan, with provisions tailored for his first marriage, gave his sons durable powers of attorney for health and financial decisions. Donna would have no legal say in the matter and she knew the sons would not include her voluntarily in their decisions. If Ted died, his will, still in effect from his first marriage, would benefit only the boys.

Ted was the optimist in the family, always expecting the best, looking for the silver lining around every dark cloud. Donna loved that about him; it balanced her own tendency to brood and worry about things she couldn't control.

A few weeks before the heart attack, Ted and Donna had consulted an estate attorney, to bring Ted's estate plan up-to-date. She had been relieved when Ted finally acknowledged her fear that she would not have financial protection if something happened to him. The papers were drafted; all they had to do was review and sign them, which Ted was planning to do the next day. Unfortunately, he never had the chance; an unexpected storm and a rickety bridge led to a chain of events beyond his control. Because a draft is not legally binding until it is signed, dated and witnessed, Donna had no protection against one of the things she feared most.

Optimism is a Mixed Blessing

Who would think that optimism, like longevity, has a downside? But it does. Optimism, which is defined as expecting the best possible outcome, sounds comforting, and is just what we want to hear when we are concerned about something. Mature optimism, however, recognizes that bad things can happen, things over which we have little or no control. It is not wishful, or naively positive, thinking. It is open and honest, and recognizes the reality of our existence. It is practical and action oriented. It's based on analysis and the long view, with a good dose of hope thrown in.

Hope is an emotion that creates a physiological reaction; it actually creates endorphins in our brain. Endorphins are the chemicals responsible for the runner's high: they give us the ability to keep doing what we're doing. Endorphins are great in the short-term because we feel so good. However, in the long run, they keep us from taking corrective steps when we should.

In this same way, our hope for a long and healthy life could cause some to overlook the need for a 'back-up' plan, should reality take a different turn. The mature optimist balances that hope with practical, protective planning.

If those who survive you are not protected - by a will, durable powers of attorney, funeral instructions, health care directives and other legal documents - they may not have the right to make decisions about your care. Their hands will be tied, and the choices that then are made on your behalf may not reflect their, or your, wishes.

These topics are a critical part of what crucial conversations are all about.

Remember:

- The only thing we can control is to plan for the things we can't control.

- Willingness to plan is an act of love.

- Confronting our death frees our children to face it too.

2 It's Not about the Money

Why We Confuse Money With Love

> "*The longest path is the one that leads*
> *from the heart to the pocket.*"
>
> Rabbi Nilton Bonder, *The Kabbalah of Money*

Consider the brevity of this chapter's explanation of money as a parallel to Rabbi Hillel's description of the Hebrew Torah. The Jewish sage summarized the message of the Book as: "Do unto others as you would have them do unto you. The rest is commentary."

Writing in more modern times, author James Buchan captures the essence of what money represents in *Frozen Desire ; The Meaning of Money* : "What is value? What you want. What is utility? What you want. What is price? What you pay in money for the above."

We're accustomed to the idea that parents will leave

their money to their children via inheritance. But we've also seen movies, read books, or known from personal experience about families gathered in the lawyer's office for the reading of the will, only to find they were left less than they expected to receive. The reading of a will can rip a family apart; relatives may feel betrayed if they don't receive the inheritance they somehow believed they would get.

What's wrong with parents wanting to leave money for their children? Or leaving part of it to them, and giving the rest to someone else? Is there such a thing as leaving too much? Should children be protected from the effects a huge inheritance can have on their life? If money is good for parents, why isn't it good for children? Should children be punished for using money in a way their parents don't approve? Is not leaving money to children punishing them?

These are not idle questions; they lie at the heart of why parents and children choose not to raise the uncomfortable issue of inheritance. The difficulty is not about 'money,' but what money has come to represent. If we take money out of the equation, how would we know that we are 'loved?' Somewhere along the historical timeline of the development of money, it became the measuring system for love in the realm of family relationships. But is bequeathing money the same as bequeathing love? How do we decide what love is worth?

In the beginning, there was no money, nor even the idea of money. There was only exchange: cows and oxen, shells and beads, furs and skins, gold and silver rings, tobacco and rice, spices and salt, tools and pots. The exchange was as simple as, "You want what I have; I want what you have." An equal exchange. Simple, clean, easy - but limited.

Enter the idea of money, a bridge between things that had previously been exchanged directly. According to anthropologists, money was first used as a convenient substitute for sacrificial animals in religious ceremonies, and for paying tribute and taxes to whoever was in charge.

Today, we're operating on the same principle, but with a lot more convenience. We've replaced whale's teeth and kettles with paper and coins, plastic and bytes. All of them are tools that facilitate exchange. They don't represent value or wealth in themselves. As Milton Friedman pointed out, "The real reason money works is that people accept it in place of goods. Why? Because they know others will. The pieces of paper are valuable because everyone thinks they are."

On the same Kenyan safari I mentioned earlier, our jeep passed a brick house built in the middle of the Masai Mara. The house belonged to the chief of the Masai tribe. Parked in the driveway were a Lexus and an SUV, and we could see a satellite receiver on the roof.

As we pulled into the village of mud huts that was part of our tour, our guide told us that no one in the village is impressed by the cars, or for that matter, anything else the chief owns. The only thing for which they envy him is the huge pile of goat dung behind the house. To a Masai, who uses dung for patching his roof, building a fire for cooking, fertilizing a small vegetable garden and various other mundane uses, a large pile of dung represents wealth. Using any portion of his dung pile as currency to obtain a car or satellite receiver makes no sense to the average Masai. None of these items hold any value for him. His 'value pile' or wealth represents his opinion that a large dung heap is more valuable than a Lexus. Distilled to its essence, the Masai agree about what represents value in their culture. Something is worth whatever we think it is worth. Because there is no way to find an objective worth for anything, worth is each person's subjective opinion. Worth is like beauty; it's in the eye of the beholder. For example, you may think it's worth it to wear designer clothes with a clearly identifiable logo. I might opt for the knock-off with no visible difference in logo or quality. It's your opinion vs. mine. Each of us is assigning subjective value to the garment.

Money is the common value system that allows us to assign a numerical unit of worth to a transaction between people. If what you think something is worth isn't what I think it's worth, we don't have a deal.

Money Isn't Natural or Neutral

There's nothing in the natural world that parallels the concept of money. We're not born knowing how to use it, nor is it coded in our DNA or wired into our autonomic system as a survival instinct. A five-year-old would as gleefully shred a hundred dollar bill into confetti as he would colored paper. We have to be taught money's value as a symbolic exchange.

At midnight on January 1, 1999, the currencies of 16 countries began their three-year conversion into a common currency called the Euro. When the newly minted notes and coins became Europe's official currency in 2002 , the money of each of the 16 countries was no longer recognized as legal currency, and so lost its value.

According to Bernard Lietaer, an economist and one of the designers of the Euro, underpinning the concept of what we call money is a shared cultural agreement. We have to agree from the beginning that what we choose to use to represent money has the value of money. The Euro is the common European currency because the 16 countries who use it agree that it is. Without our agreement, the paper or coins that represent money have no worth. The same is true for anything to which we assign value. Even sacred texts like the Torah, New Testament, and the Koran would simply be paper, without authority or validity. Without agreement, no material thing has any value, and no community undertaking has any authority. The idea that links sacred texts, money and traffic signals is this presence of cultural agreement.

The Foundations of Money

Underpinning the agreement we share about money is the idea of the promises we connect with money. Economist Harry Scherman writes in his book *The Promises Men Live By* that "there are two levels of exchange transactions. The first is the completed exchange where you buy something with the agreed upon currency. The second kind is the deferred exchange which is a promise to pay in the future for something you buy now."

In the financial world, this promise to pay in the future is typically secured by a financial contract. It can be a promissory note, a loan, a mortgage, a credit card, a bond or any other financial instrument drawn up to formalize the promise. What stands between the promise and the payment is the intention and ability of the person who made the promise.

The dictionary defines promise as "an assurance that something will certainly happen or be done." The engine of our economic system is driven by promises. When we cut through the babble of explanations by economists and behavioral scientists about the collapse of the financial system in 2008, we wind up with two facts - promises were made and promises were not kept.

In the world of relationships, the promise underlying the exchange is reciprocity: 'I treat you well; you treat me well.' Whether spelled out clearly as in marriage contracts, or implied as in family assumptions such as 'someday this will all be yours,' we're always aware, or should be, that the statement is balanced by 'if you keep your promise.' It is the promise of reciprocity that is assumed, but not kept, that creates financial conflicts in families.

First, let's define our terms. An inheritance is a material asset designated for someone specific from one generation to another. I use the term 'legacy' as the expanded sense of the word to embrace the concept of how a person is remembered. We may not have material assets to leave to our children, but we leave a legacy in spite of ourselves.

For example, when President Barack Obama nominated Tom Daschle as Secretary for Health and Human Services, everyone in Washington thought he was slated for quick approval by both houses of Congress. After rumors surfaced about his tax problems and acceptance of gifts from the private sector, specifically drug companies, Daschle withdrew as a candidate. A close friend told the media that Daschle's conflict of interest problems may have stemmed from his desire to make enough money to leave his children a generous inheritance. Instead, Daschle has left his children with a different sort of inheritance – a legacy of embarrassment.

Money as Mirror

We speak using the language of money. Our love is measured by it, as is the value of our work. The more we're paid, the more others believe in the value of what we do. If we're 'in charge' of the money, we pay ourselves what we think we're worth: if we work for someone else, they decide how much we're 'worth'. Others evaluate us based on that salary, or the trappings it provides. Unfortunately, we sometimes judge ourselves using the same measurement.

This importance that we place on money, and the values we hold personally, create our money filters, determining what we buy and to what we contribute. Others look at us through their own money filters, and assign a value to who we are. For example, for some people, associating with others who are rich validates their own self- image. When allowed into the realm of the wealthy, the glitter reflects on them, giving the illusion that they have 'made' it.

How else to explain the recent Bernard Madoff debacle, where smart and successful people were seduced into one of the greatest Ponzi schemes of all times? As one investor who lost $10 million said, "If Bernie took us on, it meant we were in the charmed inner circle."

Consider an auction a few years ago of memorabilia belonging to Bob Hope. Things he'd worn, shaved with, slept on...If this was your Uncle Harry's collection, you'd be tossing it out, having a garage sale, or donating it to the Salvation Army.

Instead, the auction of Hope's belongings began with a gala event on the September 4 Atlantic crossing of the Queen Mary 2. A sample of items on auction included: golf clubs, an Indian headdress, golf clothes, a Movado watch inscribed 'To Bob Hope in sincere appreciation — The Cleveland Press Christmas Show 1944' and a turquoise western suit made by Nudies of North Hollywood, and worn by Hope on several of his television shows. Bob Hope's ordinary memorabilia and everyday items raised millions for the Bob and Dolores Hope Charitable Foundation to support Veterans' causes.

Now consider a different scenario – the illusion of value associated with diamonds. Basically, diamonds are a collection of tiny carbon crystals that are readily mined in a number of countries around the world. The diamond's value was created over the years, through an international cartel that controlled the supply allowed onto the world market.

When diamond prices collapsed during the Depression, a clever ad campaign by N.W. Ayer, a leading advertising agency in the United States, came up with the idea of linking diamonds to love. The larger the diamond, the greater the love. This romanticizing of diamonds was a huge success, instilling in the modern consciousness of young men and women that a diamond engagement ring means 'real' love and is a prerequisite to marriage. Can he really love you without a diamond? Can he have you without giving you a diamond? Is the diamond large enough? If he can't afford to buy you the diamond you want, can you still love him?

These may seem like frivolous questions; in actuality, they are indicators of money seeping into a decision about love and marriage. Your own value system will determine if the size of the diamond matches the declaration of love.

Tiffany runs full page ads showing a diamond ring with the caption 'A Diamond is Forever.' Capitalizing on our increasing longevity, and heralding marriages that survive more than a few years, the 'Anniversary Diamond' is featured with the caption "Show her you'd do it all over again." Love has become inextricably linked to this cluster of carbon, that has no intrinsic value other than the high cost we agree to pay for it.

"Price is what you pay. Value is what you get" says Warren Buffett. In all of these cases, we're creating the perception of value where none exists. If we took money out of the equation, how would we know that we love? Somewhere along the line, in the realm of family relationships, money became a measuring system for love.

Remember:

- Money is a blank screen upon which we project our values.
- Wealth and abundance are not equivalent.
- No one knows how much love is worth.

3 Why We Need Crucial Conversations

Removing the Taboos of Touchy Subjects

Ayear after being widowed, Patty Lawson, age 72, met Bill Carr, a retired airline pilot. When their relationship blossomed and they decided to marry, she sold her home and invested the proceeds in a new house she and Bill were building together. Like many people, her home represents Patty's primary asset; she and her first husband focused on raising and assisting their three girls, and so only managed to 'put away' a little. For this reason, she hasn't worried about a will or trust.

Bill does have other assets, including a pension and investments, that provide enough regular income to support him and Patty. He also has children from his first marriage. Years ago, Bill set up a will and trust to make sure they would be provided for after he dies. He also drew up papers giving his kids durable powers of attorney for health and financial matters in case something happens to him.

But this was all arranged before Bill met Patty, so she isn't included as a beneficiary of the trust. If Bill dies, or is incapacitated, her only asset will be her half interest in their home. Since the house they built lost almost 40 percent of its value during the recession of 2008, she may end up looking to her children for financial help. Unfortunately, Patty's children are nearing their own retirement; they are feeling the stress of having to help their own children, and have never considered that their mother may need assistance as well.

Fortunately, Bill and Patty have enjoyed good health for most of their lives. Even though they're approaching their 80s, they still feel young and vital. They haven't spent money on long-term care insurance; they've used the money to travel and take cruises instead. So, what will happen to Patty and Bill, should one of them suddenly take ill and require long-term care? Most likely, they would need to liquidate some of Bill's assets... the same assets Bill's children believe will one day be available to them.

And so it goes: the choices of one generation clearly impacting the lives of another - yet with no one talking about the potential consequences. If Bill, Patty and their children don't talk about what they expect (or even worse, what they *don't* expect) and how to plan for it, everyone in this situation will suffer.

Why do we procrastinate until it's too late to have the crucial conversations we need to have? Why are death and inheritance so hard to talk about?

Social custom teaches us that it's rude and insensitive to pry into other people's financial affairs, or to raise subjects that will make them uncomfortable. Death and money are to us what sex was to the Victorians; uncomfortable and impolite to discuss, but with repercussions that make conversation necessary. The culture of silence around these issues results in countless unnecessary complications, and pain for millions of families.

Home Instead Senior Care, a national provider of home care services, created a formula for this very important conversation – the '40-70 Rule.' It means that children who have reached age 40, or whose parents have reached age 70, need to start discussions to outline expectations and responsibilities regarding living arrangements, health concerns, driving privileges, and financial matters. A survey by the company showed that death itself doesn't seem to be the taboo subject; it's a reluctance to talk about things that might upset their family that presents the greater challenge for older parents.

The reluctance to talk goes both ways. Boomers don't want to be perceived as greedy or impolite if they raise the subject of their parents' financial resources and inheritance. They don't want to intrude on their parents' privacy and autonomy, or be perceived as waiting for their parents to die.

Their parents are often more willing to discuss end-of-life issues, but are fearful of the emotional minefield of inheritance disclosure to children. Even though they know it's important that their children aren't surprised by the content of their wills, parents still hesitate to initiate conversations about their plans.

George Johnson is 78-years-old, and a two generation grandfather. He married at 21, raised five children and has seven grandchildren from his first marriage. After a divorce, he remarried. He and his second wife have two daughters together, and three additional grandchildren.

George has helped both sets of children financially and some continue to need it. He's reluctant to get everyone together to talk about his will and estate plan because he helped some family members more than others and doesn't want them to think he plays favorites. George watches his assets decrease and worries that his children may have to take care of him. "Pretty soon I may not remember any of their names. That should solve the problem," he jokes wryly.

Longevity Changes Everything

It's never been more important for parents and adult children to talk about finances, health decisions, estate planning, and end-of-life care. Parents are living longer, and increasingly needing assisted care in their 'twilight years.' While they may not want to change the family dynamic by looking to their children for assistance, they have to be realistic about the possibility they may need it. Children need, and have the right, to know about this possibility, so they can plan such help into their own financial lives.

Broaching such topics, especially with aging parents who consider their finances none of the kids' business, can cause everyone difficulties, often eliciting feelings of anger, frustration and offense. Parents may also feel a sense of guilt or shame that they even require financial help from their children. It's no surprise that most people avoid it.

However, it's unfair and counterproductive for parents not to welcome a discussion about their finances, their wills, their medical needs and arrangements, end-of-life wishes and funeral preferences. Not talking about these subjects won't help anyone. Aging and death don't go away just because we don't start the conversation.

We can't read each other's mind. We don't know what other people want unless they tell us.

For example, my neighbor Margo says that she can't even broach the subject of end-of-life planning with her two sons in their forties. One of them is a lawyer; the other runs a manufacturing business. "It's absurd. Two well-educated men who are still avoiding what they know must happen some day," she says. "I want them to know I want cremation and I don't want a funeral service. I want them to scatter my ashes at sea and then invite my friends to a big party to celebrate my life, with all my favorite music and especially, Frank Sinatra singing "My Way.""

After trying several times to initiate conversations, Margo gave up talking about it. Instead, she wrote out in detail what she wants, had her instructions notarized, and sent copies to her sons, her doctor and lawyer. That was two years ago, and her sons still haven't discussed the letters with her.

Families today are different and more complicated than they were even fifty years ago. Social changes such as later marriage, later childbearing, later divorce, remarriage and second families mean that men and women are older when they enter these family roles.

Millions of children of boomer parents have become reluctant to leave home or are returning home before launching into their own adulthood. Partly the result of a tough economy and tight job market, this generation of young adults is taking far longer to claim their adult-hood, marry and function on their own without their parent's financial help. Boomer parents are caring for children from infancy to the mid-twenties or later, while their own parents, in their 80s and 90s, may also need their help.

As they get ready for their own retirement, baby boomers, often referred to as 'The Sandwich Generation,' are squeezed between the needs and demands of people they love – their parents and their children. It's a heavy burden, made harder to bear by widespread silence on the subject. The result is a lack of clarity, honesty and readiness for what will inevitably happen.

Both generations perpetuate this conspiracy of silence about death. Adult children don't want to accept the possibility that a sick parent is really going to die. Parents don't want to talk about it because they don't want to face it themselves.

No one is well served by this reluctance to talk: longevity has changed the rules. If children are reluctant to talk, parents need to find other ways to detail their wishes, as Margo did. Likewise, if parents don't want to discuss end-of-life issues, their finances, their funeral wishes, their health or anything else their children need to know, the children have not only the right to broach the subject, but the duty to do so.

Sheila and her two sisters send money to their 85-year-old mother every month. Their mother owns the house they grew up in, but needs the additional money to supplement her monthly social security income. However, when Sheila asks her mother for information about her will, her end-of-life wishes and her medical care, information that she and her sisters should have, her mother takes offense at 'the kids butting into her life.'

Sheila says, "We're tempted not to send more money

until we get the information we need. None of us want to be the 'bad guy,' cutting off money to our mom, but how are we supposed to plan ahead or step in and help without the information we need to have?"

Boomer Children in the Dark about Aging Parents

Brian Carpenter, an assistant professor of psychology at Washington University in St. Louis, researches intergenerational communication about parental lifestyle preferences and end-of-life issues. His findings show that a stranger might have the same chance at correctly predicting parental wishes as their own children would. He also concludes that two adult siblings may have radically different views on what their parents would want in their later years.

One question Carpenter and his colleagues seek answers to is: What makes children good at predicting parental responses to parental lifestyle preferences?

"Currently, there is no clear indicator of which children will be 'good' predictors, nor which ones will be 'bad' predictors of their parents' lifestyle preferences," he says. "While there is some evidence that children who perceive their relationships as emotionally closer are better predictors, there seems to be no significant correlation between gender, age or geographical proximity of children and parents and whether or not a child is a 'good' or 'poor' predictor of parental wishes."

Why should any child be put into a situation of predicting parental wishes? What a huge responsibility for parents to shunt off on their children - one that is widely complicated by the possibility of friction with other siblings. Why would anyone cede those decisions to their loved ones if they had the chance to discuss them before an emergency happened? Isn't it better for both generations to talk about what they want and put it in writing?

For example, in the Terri Schiavo case, determining what a loved one would want was neither a simple nor clear decision. The young woman was left in a persistent vegetative state after having a cardiac arrest. Unconscious and sustained by artificial hydration and nutrition through a feeding tube, Terri was unable to speak for herself. Because she had no official medical directive, her husband Michael, who argued that she would not have wanted to be kept alive in this fashion, was locked into a 15 year battle with her parents, who refused to allow the withdrawal of the life sustaining technologies.

"When you're at that moment, when you have to say, 'Yes, let's discontinue life support,' that's really challenging psychologically, no matter what your beliefs were before that moment," says Carpenter. "That's the one case that made the news, but these kinds of decisions get made every day."

I wrote the following for KQED, the public radio station in San Francisco, during the Terry Schiavo controversy. I had heard stories of too many families who, like the Schiavos, had no written directive regarding medical care and end-of-life issues. I didn't want my daughters to have to guess about what I want when I die.

What This Mom Wants When She Dies

I'm too young to own a grave, but I bought one anyway. It's located on a grassy knoll next to an oak tree, with a wraparound view of the hills that I love. I bought it during a special sale and paid for it with my credit card. I laughed as I made plans to

44

apply the card's frequent flier miles for an upgrade to business class on my next hiking trip to Italy.

You might think, "This lady is crazy. There must be other ways to add frequent flier miles than buying a gravesite." And, of course, there are. But none as loving or satisfying as knowing that, when I die, my girls aren't going to wonder, 'What did Mom want?' They won't have to disagree or create bad feelings between them at a time when they will need the love and support they can give each other.

Being able to talk about death is liberating, not morbid, for us. My daughters find it comforting that, in the normal course of events, I will die before them. Of course they will miss me. They love me as I love them. We appreciate the special gift of time spent together, creating new memories to add to the ones we already cherish.

In a sense, we're living on the other side of goodbye. I've written my end-of-life preferences out for them. Everything is signed and dated: a medical directive in case I can't make my own medical decisions and durable powers of attorney if they have to act on my behalf with financial decisions. My will is up–to-date. My daughters know how they will share my financial assets. There won't be any surprises for them that might jeopardize their relationship with each other.

I'd like to live to 100 years. These days, that could happen. But if I die sooner, my children will always know that I loved and respected them enough to take responsibility for the end of my days. Meanwhile, I'll enjoy finding other ways to add to my frequent flier miles.

The vast majority of people will, at some point, be involved in parent care. Families must talk about the aging issues they might face before a crisis arises. These conversations are not easy for families to have, but they will help avert problems and conflicts in their future.

Unintended Consequences

On the face of it, longevity is a blessing. Don't we all want to live as long as we can? Don't we want to have our relationships with people we love for as long as possible? In reality, the longevity revolution is turning out to be a mixed blessing for future generations.

The fastest growing segment of the population today is seniors over 85-years-old. Researchers at Boston University, who are studying New England centenarians, estimate that three million baby boomers will reach age 100. Just run the numbers: 75 million baby boomers, of whom three million are projected to live to 100.

This is a huge change from just 100 years ago, when reaching age 50 was considered an accomplishment. Back then, it was not uncommon for families to lose several children to sickness. Today, childhood diseases are mostly under control, allowing for a longer average lifespan. In addition, medical advances have also made it possible for those who do live past childhood to expect to live a very long time.

Thanks to improvements in prevention of, and intervention for, adult diseases like high blood pressure, diabetes, heart disease and cancer, the average life expectancy has climbed to 80 years for women, 74 for men. But though the age has increased, not all of those years will be spent in good health - and even when the health of an aged parent is not an issue, the decreased ambulatory capacities that are a natural part of life in one's 80s means a need for additional care. That means there's a good chance that baby boomers will spend more time than most planned for helping their aging parents.

For nearly four decades, baby boomers have heard about the inheritance windfall: the billions of dollars that would cascade from their parents' generation to them. What no one counted on was how longevity, made possible by advances in medical technology and healthy lifestyle changes in the senior population, would impact that inheritance.

At a time when baby boomers are looking forward to their own retirement, they're now confronted with two major changes that impact their plans. The first is the longevity revolution, and its effect on their parents and themselves. The second is the increasing tendency of their own adult children to delay embracing full financial responsibility for their life.

Today, more than 25 percent of American families are involved in some way with parental care. For many, the responsibility of caring for aging parents hits at the same time they are also helping put their children through college.

Add to that the large numbers of young people in their twenties and thirties who continue to rely on their parents for financial support. No wonder Boomers feel wedged between two generations; they have both older and younger family members who simultaneously need their support and care. No one has any idea how these trends will play out. And so far, there are no long-term social plans to deal with either of them.

But they will need to be dealt with - a look at the statistics makes that abundantly clear:

A Putnam Investments Survey in 2006 estimated that nearly 30 million working adults, age 45 or older, have at least one living parent, and about one-fifth (or 6.2 million people) provide financial support on average of $240 a month for their parents.

Another group in the survey is working adults, age 45 or older, with at least one child 25 or older. Of these 23.5 million adults, about one in four are either housing (20%) or writing a rent check for (4%) grown children.

The long-term cost of providing financial support for grown children is high. Forty-three percent of parents who help their kids financially expect it will force them back to work after retirement; 38% expect to save less, threatening their standard of living in their retirement, and 29% anticipate delaying retirement altogether.

Despite these financial hardships imposed by the need to help parents or grown children, 57% of those supporting parents said they were "very pleased" to make the sacrifice, and 38% of parents supporting a grown child felt the same way.

When asked what financial lessons were learned from providing support to elderly parents, adult children surveyed said they would have saved money specifically to support their parents, would have bought long-term care insurance for them, and should use a professional advisor to plan their own retirement. However, asked if financial support for parents or adult children was included in their planning, 70% of parents supporting adult children said it came as a surprise.

Another survey, conducted that same year by Roper Public Affairs of more than 1,000 seniors and adult children, concluded that generations perceive aging issues differently.

A major finding was that seniors are more comfortable than their adult children talking about aging issues; they just aren't comfortable talking about it *with* their children. On the other hand, adult children want to have these conversations, but they don't want to be the ones to initiate them.

Situations can become particularly difficult in blended, multi-marriage families, where new spouses and step-children can leave children from previous relationships disinherited, often unintentionally. In families where a widowed parent has begun a relationship with someone new, family members worry what impact this person will have on the family's future when it comes to inheritance issues.

As long as the parents are alive, these conflicts between family members often remain under wraps. Family advisers suggest that parents who want to prevent conflict in the family, especially after they die, should suggest holding a family conference. Parents can lay out their plans - everything from where their wills are to how they've invested their assets - and explain their rationale in the presence of all concerned parties.

This kind of discussion is more art than science, and can be even trickier if parents intend to distribute assets unequally among their children. Involving an outsider - a lawyer, counselor, financial adviser or even a family friend – is often a good idea. This person can calmly direct the conversation, and mediate if and when tensions arise.

So, while contemplating these conversations may make you feel uncomfortable, or raise fears of conflict with other family members, the earlier you start the conversations, the better. In the last chapter of this book, you will find guidelines for discussion between you and your family. You need to make these crucial conversations a priority.

Remember:

- There is no right time to talk. There is only 'in time.'
- No one can read your mind.
- No subject is taboo if it affects your life.
- If you don't say what you need, you won't get it.

4 Someday, This Will All Be Yours

Money, Inheritance and the Trouble with Feeling Entitled

> *"Life is not fair: get used to it."*
>
> Bill Gates

When Leona Helmsley, hotel magnate dubbed 'Queen of Mean' by the media, died, her will left $12 million for the care of her dog, Trouble, who will be buried near her in her mausoleum. She left nothing to two of her four grandchildren, citing "reasons which are known to them."

Helmsley was not known for her compassion or generosity as an employer. Yet, she bequeathed most of her estimated $4 billion estate to her charitable trust, which was set up in 1999 to benefit religious and educational causes, groups that work to protect children, and other charities in New York City.

People were outraged that she chose her dog over two of her grandchildren. Her thinking about her will may have been simple: 'My dog loves me, is good to me, and I feel appreciated. I don't want to reward my grandchildren for treating me badly. I'll leave money for the other two.'

Unless the grandchildren provide more details about their relationship with their grandmother, we're not likely to know Helmsley's real reason for disinheriting them.

Few people realize that of all the countries in the world, only England and the United States give parents 'testamentary freedom,' the right to designate who shall inherit their estate, sometimes to the exclusion of their children. In other countries, although the percentage varies, children are always entitled to some portion of a parent's estate.

In the United States then, because children and grandchildren are not automatically entitled to any portion of their parents' estate, anything they do receive is because parents choose to leave it to them. In Helmsley's case, her relationship with her dog apparently gave her more pleasure, companionship and love than she received from her children or grandchildren. Sad, selfish, eccentric, mean spirited…possibly. You and I might not do it, but it's her money and this is America.

Because of testamentary freedom, the relationship between parents and children provides the bedrock for inheritance; what is customary is not the law. Inheritance may initially have been Biblically inspired, but primogeniture, the right of the first-born son to claim everything, is history. So, except for the state of

Louisiana, which still operates under Napoleonic laws of inheritance instituted in the 19th century, inheritance in the United States lies not in the genes, but in the heart.

If I Can Do It, You Can Do It

A nationwide study by PNC Financial Services Group in 2005 showed that half of survey respondents with children at home worry that their kids will grow up feeling entitled. Of adults with more than $1 million in investable assets, 44% believe their children are spoiled, and nine out of 10 agree that it is important for children to learn the value of money through hard work. This survey also found that more than half of respondents have never discussed these opinions on entitlement with their children.

Parents who earned rather than inherited their wealth are more likely to adopt an 'I-earned-it-now-you-earn-it-too' approach, that bucks the sense of entitlement many children have about their parents' wealth.

Bill Cosby tells the story of shopping with his son, who nagged him to buy a new electronic gadget. Cosby told him it was too expensive and that he couldn't have it. His son said "Why not, Dad? We're rich." Cosby answered, "Your mother and I are rich, son; you're not." Knowing Cosby and his attitudes about children, he successfully nipped entitlement in the bud.

On the surface, it may sound noble to say that children will have to make their own way in the world, and not expect to 'sponge' off their parents. It smacks of that yeoman spirit that encourages us to stand on our own two feet, commit ourselves to a plan and goal, and make it happen without expecting handouts.

Some well-known people think like that. Anita Roddick, founder of the Body Shop, died in 2004 without passing a penny of her fortune to her two daughters. She is quoted in the London Times as saying that 'leaving money to your family is obscene.' Roddick wanted her fortune to go towards green issues and helping to cure Third World problems that had been a major goal of her life's work.

Warren Buffett doesn't believe that money equates with love. He wants his children to carve out their own place in the world. He believes that setting them up "with a lifetime supply of food stamps just because they came out of the right womb can be harmful for them and is an antisocial act." After putting his two sons and a daughter through college, Buffett gave each of them seed money to launch and run their own charitable foundations. Beyond that, says his daughter Susan, "if I write my dad a check for $20, he cashes it."

Nigela Lawson, author and TV cooking personality in England, and her husband Charles Saatchi are estimated to have a combined net worth of 110 million English pounds. They disagree on what they should leave their children. Lawson, an Oxford graduate who was raised in a privileged home, believes that her children shouldn't be handed financial security. "It ruins people not having to earn money," she is quoted as saying.

Jason Connery won't inherit a penny of his actor father's 84 million pound estate. Sean Connery cites his philosophy that his son should make his own way and fortune, without having the luxury of dropping his famous father's name or using a fortune he didn't earn. Connery says he was brought up the hard way. It worked for him and he expects it to work for his son.

Children of the famous have lots of company. A 2005

Allianz American Legacies Study about attitudes towards inheritance found that 54% of elders believe in some form of 'performance-based inheritance.' They think a child deserves more if he or she provides care for the parent or makes their life easier. For example, the child who accompanies them to the doctor, takes them to the bank or helps them in other hands-on ways is demonstrating a level of sensitivity and caring that parents appreciate as they age. Similarly, one-third think children deserve less if they cause conflict or disrespect the family. The nationwide survey showed that 45% of high net worth and 23% of lower net worth elders do not feel that all children have the right to share equally in their inheritance.

"I don't believe in equality," says Molly Donahue, 74, a retired accountant and mother of two daughters, who lives in San Diego. "I treat my children as individuals, not equals." Although she plans to split her assets between the two, she will distribute some prized personal items as she sees fit, not based on their actual monetary value. She has told her daughters about her intentions and they seem fine with it. What Molly can't control is how they will react to her decisions after she is gone. "I'm not worried about that. You can only do what you can do. Once I'm gone, they'll have to work it out," she says.

The idea of unequal distribution flies in the face of a basic tenet of parenting, namely that parents love and treat their children equally. The polarization over inheritance concerns two opposing principles. On the one hand is meritocracy: how hard we work to earn what we receive. It's how we get ahead at school, land a solid job, and get promoted. On the other hand is the concept of equality, of loving each child equally. When it comes to the transfer of family wealth, the two principles often oppose each other.

Ken Dychtwald, gerontologist and CEO of Age Wave, a consulting firm in San Francisco, says that we accept meritocracy on the football team or at work, but somehow we've held inheritance to a loftier, altruistic ideal, where inheritance by merit should not be considered. "It used to be a formula: the oldest son got the farm, and the oldest daughter got a dowry," says Dychtwald. "In the 20th Century we moved to a more equal distribution as the accepted norm. Now there is no clear prescription. Parents are trying to reach Solomon-like decisions in their giving."

Today, incentive provision clauses are being added to wills, requiring that children be productive members of society in order to receive their full inheritance. Another increasingly popular clause is one that leaves a child an annual amount equal to what he or she earns in employment—but not a penny more. One estate planner calls this attempt to encourage meritocracy 'the make-a-dollar-get-a-dollar model.'

Mark Elliott, an 80-year-old father in Boston, is still torn about the inheritance he is leaving his three sons. The youngest, by his candid description, "fritters his life away, drinking it up, getting involved with strange women." Mark gave serious thought to decreasing that son's share. "I talked myself out of it. He's still my son, and that wouldn't be fair. I just hope he sees the error of his ways," he says.

"There's a strong culture of equality that's deeply embedded in the American character," says Paul Schervish, director of the Center on Wealth and Philanthropy at Boston College. "The problem is whether merit and equality can coexist when it comes to inheritance."

This dilemma is causing parents I know great stress and heartache. Les and Tricia have two sons. Jim is a successful doctor who worked his way through medical school. John is affectionately known as the 'family slouch.' The parents decided to will Jim less money, because he doesn't really need it, and leave more to John whose financial future looks shaky. However, they're wondering if it's fair to, in effect, punish Jim for being successful while rewarding John for having little ambition. On the other hand, would it be fair to give them both equal shares, when one may have a greater need throughout his life?

It's easy to understand why parents feel so conflicted: children are apt to take a parent's will as a final report card.

According to Steven Hendlin, PhD., a clinical psychologist and author of *Overcoming the Inheritance Taboo*, a high sense of entitlement is one of the defining characteristics of the baby-boomer generation, and it influences beliefs about what we deserve. It goes deeper than money; it goes to love. If one child feels less loved, it can destroy relationships.

"Most children have an expectation of some inheritance. And therein lies the real problem. We view inheritance as a birthright, because we're taught that love means giving," he writes. "That's why inheritance will always be a hot-button issue, because it's highly emotional."

Hendlin argues in his book that the sign of a healthy and mature adult is the ability to give up any expectation of inheritance of any kind. "Children could be liberated from psychological suffering if they would just let go of the infantile wish to be taken care of forever by parents," he writes.

No One is Entitled to Anything

Have you heard the joke about the CEO who insisted on moving to the front of the line at the airline counter? Asked to wait his turn by the ticket agent, he said loudly, "Do you know who I am?" The ticket agent called out to the other people in line, "Does anyone know who this gentleman is?"

Entitlement is a one-way mindset, a pattern of focusing on what we are owed in all relationships without awareness of our own obligations. Children raised with entitlement, rather than learning a sense of personal responsibility, believe the world revolves around them. They receive a legacy about how to live, whether we intend it or not; they are disabled from functioning productively in the real world.

We're surrounded by messages of entitlement - from The Declaration of Independence ('life, liberty and the pursuit of happiness') to L'Oreal hair coloring ('costs a little more, but I'm worth it'). The truth is that we're not really entitled to anything.

We may *feel* entitled in certain situations. When expectations aren't met in a defined reciprocal relationship, we often get irritated or angry. For example, I feel entitled to courtesy and good service when I choose to buy something. The rude hotel or airline clerk, the inattentive waiter, and the repairman who shows up three hours late are not doing their job. These are minor examples, but I'm really annoyed when someone does not keep their end of the bargain. If I do something nice for someone, I want to be thanked. Maybe it's old-fashioned to be thanked for holding a door open, but I don't like to be taken for granted, especially in situations that don't require that I take any action.

Entitlement, the notion that just because 'we are who

we are' means that we deserve special treatment, is a learned response. It begins in childhood when too much is given and too little asked in return.

My friends Tom and Lois Bradford experienced this recently. When their daughter Holly lost a substantial part of her portfolio during the 2008 financial downturn, she could no longer afford to send her own daughters to horseback riding camp, as she had promised for the following summer.

Tom and Lois had reservations on a three-week cruise which they had planned for over a year. Holly asked them to cancel their cruise, and use the funds so their grandchildren could attend horseback riding camp. Tom and Lois declined, saying they had planned this vacation for a long time. Holly accused them of selfishness, saying they could go on a cheaper cruise and use the difference for their grandchildren's camp.

Lois was appalled at her daughter's request, and realized that this wasn't the first time she and Tom had been confronted with Holly's sense of entitlement. Lois suggested that this would be a good time to break the pattern for another generation. She told her daughter to explain to the grandchildren that they couldn't afford camp this year. Holly responded with "Yes, and I'll tell them their grandparents chose to spend the money on themselves instead of helping you go to camp."

From Investment to Love Object

During the six decades between 1870 to 1930, a huge transformation took place in how American parents regarded their children.

Viviana Zelizer, a social historian, writes in her book *Pricing the Priceless Child : The Changing Social Value of Children*, about the transformation of children from economic asset that helped support the family, to an object of love around which the family was organized.

The influx of immigrants during these decades provided a new source of labor for factories, and social reformers began to define child labor as a moral problem. The political movement they created resulted in compulsory education for all children and restrictive labor laws. Eventually, the movement against child labor spread from the urban middle class to the farms. By the late 1930s, children began to be valued for their emotional return-on-investment rather than for their economic contribution.

In the decades since then, cultural and social changes have resulted in children often becoming the only permanent love relationships people have. Geographic mobility has often severed ties with siblings and parents. One-third of marriages and half of second marriages in the United States end in divorce. Male or female, people are much more likely to have a permanent relationship with their children than with a spouse.

With time, the child has became the center around which the family unit is organized. Parents place more emphasis on providing their children with 'a better life' and in exchange, expect a greater emotional return on their investment. Modern children expect to receive things; when they don't, they feel less loved. Parents expect to receive love and appreciation: when they don't, they feel resentful.

Parents didn't always feel guilty about how they raised their children. They didn't know they could have done 'a better job.' They did what they thought they should, considering themselves lucky if their children survived childhood. They were more concerned with respect for their authority than expressions of love.

Today, we have an enormous emotional investment in our children. We want to give them a better childhood than we had: we want them to be happy, successful and serve as our cushion of immortality. Raising them is probably the most expensive thing most people will ever do. The latest figures show that families making $70,200 a year or more will spend nearly $270,000 to raise a child from birth through age 17. Parents invest the money gladly, not really thinking about it until they feel hurt, unloved or taken for granted by the children. It's the lack of reciprocity, the insensitivity and attitude of entitlement that triggers parents' resolve to rein in their generosity.

Fair Versus Equal

My late husband's will stipulated that the business he founded go to his eldest son, who had been employed as an engineer in the company since his graduation from college. His younger son had not graduated from high school, and had repeatedly had trouble keeping a job. My husband struggled with conflicting desires: he wanted to leave something for his younger son, but wanted him to demonstrate first that he wouldn't fritter it away. He was wrestling with how to motivate his son when he died.

He never considered an equal inheritance for the boys, but had never been able to resolve the question of fairness. In the years after my husband died, the older son successfully built the business. Did he take care of his younger brother in the process? Did he do what was 'right,' whatever that means? How did he justify the inequity to himself? Did he think it was fair because the company was his responsibility and he was doing all the work? Or did it fall into the cliché of 'What's fair is what I think I should get?'

I don't know the outcome; I have not stayed in touch with the boys. I hope that the older son made some sort of arrangement for his brother. It's ironic that one brother had to deal with the same unanswered questions his father struggled with.

It's very hard for parents to deal with the emotional implications of fair versus equal. No matter what they decide, they can't control how the children will respond to their decisions after they die. We've all heard bitter stories of hopes and promises being crushed when the will is finally read.

Parents have to decide for themselves what they want to leave to their children. Some believe that their children should inherit everything. The conflict for them may be between equal or non-equal distribution, not whether their children should be the sole beneficiaries. Others believe that they have already taken care of their children by providing a good childhood and college education. They might decide to skip a generation and leave their estate to their grandchildren. Many want to direct their assets to charities they believe can make the world a better place. And still others live by the mantra reflected on their bumper stickers that read, "I'm spending my children's inheritance."

I don't believe in surprises. I think that if you're feeling good about how to distribute your assets, you should share that information with your children. If you're feeling conflicted about what to do, you should let your children know that. Call a family meeting to discuss decisions you've made about inheritance and why you made them, especially if you're planning an unequal distribution of your estate.

The most important thing to consider is that no family member should be surprised when a will is read. It's better for your children's future relationship if everyone clearly understands why parents decided the way they did. This assumes that parents have thought through their decision and have reasons they can explain to their children. How children accept a parent's decision is how they always did. Those who feel entitled believed that all through their life. Why would anyone expect them to change their attitude now?

Remember:

- Inheritance is not a legal obligation.
- No one is entitled to anything.
- Inheritance is about relationship.
- Inheritance is not automatic.

5 *The Landscape of Aging*

Thinking about Your Parents' Death; Thinking About Your Own

> *"All would live long, but none would be old"*
>
> Benjamin Franklin

Every parent knows what it is to be young; no younger person knows what it is to be old. Adult children can't even imagine that one day, they will inhabit the physical and emotional terrain their parents live in. That old saying 'first you do, then you know' is very apt here. Until we experience what it's like to be old, we can't fully understand why our parents act the way they do.

One of the reasons for having crucial conversations *now* is that 'old' could happen at any time. A stroke could render a relatively young parent helpless; an accident could result in needing assisted care; early onset of

Alzheimer's disease could rob a parent of the ability to understand, or even recognize, their children.

Mary Pipher, in her book *Another Country: Navigating the Emotional Terrain of Our Elders*, describes old age as 'a foreign country, a place with a language and culture unknown to their children.' This unfamiliarity is creating a generational chasm that can make the elderly feel isolated and misunderstood while their baby boomer children, trying to care for them, feel frustrated and unappreciated.

In the decade since Pipher's book was published, the number of people age 65 and older has increased by 10 percent. They now have an average life expectancy of an additional two decades. This group constitutes 13 percent of the U.S. population. By 2020, they, along with their boomer children, will be drawing social security and receiving Medicare benefits.

Years ago, I attended a workshop designed to help boomers understand some of the physical challenges of aging. One of the exercises was for participants to open their 'aging kit' that contained earplugs, glasses with smudges on the lens, rubber gloves, keys and a pencil.

Our instructions were to insert the earplugs, put on the glasses and rubber gloves, pick up the pencil and keys and move them from hand to hand. I found myself in an unfamiliar world. My vision was blurred, I couldn't hear people around me and my fingers felt fat and uncoordinated. I couldn't move the pencil and keys from one hand to the other without them falling on the floor. When we finished the process, we shared our experience of frustration as we struggled with impaired hearing and vision, and attempted to keep items from falling out of our hands. For most of us, it was an eye-opener about what some older people experience on a sustained basis.

Bernice Neugarten, a noted gerontologist, says there is a difference between the 'young' old (65- to 74 -years old), and the 'old' old (75- to 85-years old). What distinguishes one group from the other is health, mental clarity, physical independence, and social interaction, that when combined, allows them to function on their own. What they have in common are losses, some visible to others, some not.

Long before senses dull, the young old experience losses. Sometimes, the loss is slow: the run becomes a jog, the jog a walk, the walk a shuffle. Retirement means an adjustment of identity. The older driver who surrenders her car keys and now waits for her children to drive her to the doctor, the beauty salon and her bridge group. The recreational pilot who can no longer pass his physical and gives up a life-long hobby. A bridge partner and a friend dies; then another...and another. Cumulatively, the losses mount, strength diminishes, energy lags.

A single event can bring normal life to a halt. Cleaning the gutters can result in a fall and a broken hip. A heart attack requires a complete change in lifestyle and brings long postponed plans to a halt. A spouse dies leaving the grieving survivor at greater risk of impaired immunity and subsequent illness.

These life altering events are unpredictable. Diminished options lead to increased fears. Will I become a burden to my children? Will I outlive my money? Will they put me in a nursing home? Is my money safe? Will I die alone?

Oddly enough, these are the same things their boomer children will fear as they age. "Death is the least of my worries," says 84-year-old Gloria, one of the regulars at the local Senior Center, "When my husband dies, if I run out of money, I'll drive my car off a cliff."

Unfortunately, that's not so easy to do, especially if they've taken away your car keys.

The Emotional Terrain of Aging

"I have only what I remember," writes W.S. Merwin, winner of the 2008 Nobel Prize for poetry, "The present is one moment beyond the past...and we never finish our conversation with relationships."

We carry so much life within us, so much history. As we age, we enter uncharted territory, disbelieving that we are finally here and wondering for how long. The future is tomorrow, not next year. We no longer dwell on what we don't have yet. We ruminate about how we lived our life, what it meant, to ourselves and to others.

Priorities begin to shift. Wanting to control what they can, elders begin the process gerontologists call 'life review.' How will they be remembered by the people they care about? What are their regrets? What could they have done differently?

If it's true that we are indeed what we remember, then as we age, we cling even more to our memories. Psychologists and neurophysiologists tell us that we are selective in what we remember, choosing recollections to highlight about ourselves based on keeping our self-image intact.

We begin our parenting journey with the best of intentions for our children. We seek to instill in them our values, and enable them to make their way in the world without the need to rely on us. I've never heard of anyone who intends to cause their children pain, anger, disappointment, resentment, rejection, humiliation or any of the other negative emotions that so many children attribute to their parents.

The reality is that we make mistakes as parents, mistakes often caused by misunderstandings that reach epic proportions because we don't recognize them as mistakes until much later.

The older we get, the harder it is to access why we feel the way we do. We live by rules taught to us by parents just as imperfect as we are. We wonder about this person who once was familiar to us, the young person trapped inside the aging body.

How Will You Be Remembered?

What if you awoke tomorrow morning to read your own obituary? What if, instead of correcting the mistake, you allowed it to run its course, giving you the rare opportunity to see how you are remembered?

That's exactly what happened on April 13, 1888 to Alfred Nobel, the Swedish inventor who amassed a fortune with the invention and manufacture of dynamite, nitroglycerine and gunpowder.

The obituary, printed under the headline, 'The Merchant of Death is Dead,' was the result of a French reporter's error (he was writing about Alfred's brother Albert, who had died). Horrified at being portrayed as a destructive force in the world, Alfred vowed to change his image. He left his nine million dollar fortune to fund awards for those whose work would benefit humanity, not destroy it.

Few of us will get a chance to write our own obituary. Even fewer will get the chance to read it. However, whether we realize it or not, our legacy is being shaped by the values we hold, and how those values are reflected in the life we live.

Crucial conversations between generations will help with the issues of money and inheritance. But money is only a part of legacy, that also includes values, ethics, memories, personal possessions, life lessons, wishes and instructions. Most of all, legacy deals with how we want to be remembered.

When I lived in the Midwest many years ago, there was a story about a developer of shopping malls who was stalled in his efforts to break ground on his latest project. A portion of the land was still owned by 76-year- old Ernesto Petrini, whose family had farmed that acreage for three generations. Mr. Petrini wanted his children to inherit the land and home. The community considered him a village elder and benefactor.

The developer kept raising his dollar offer for the property. Petrini kept turning him down. With mounting pressure from his investors, the developer decided to call in a mediator to deal with 'the tough old bird.'

Shortly after the mediator met with the patriarch, he emerged from the meeting with a solution. What happened in that meeting? The mediator learned that Petrini didn't want the family history 'swallowed up' by a shopping mall, with no trace of what his family had accomplished over three generations. The mediator suggested that the developer call the shopping mall Petrini Corners. Shoppers entering the mall would see a photo history of the land and the family in a special display - a win for Petrini, his family and the developer. .

The deal was concluded the following day.

What was really happening here? Mr. Petrini had more than enough money for his family; his concern was how he would be remembered for a lifetime's work. While he knew that the revenue created by the mall would be good for the future of the town nearby, the pull of his personal legacy was greater. When the mediator found a way to honor both the legacy and the need for development, the old man was satisfied.

There is a chilling folktale dating back to 14th century Europe that illustrates what we teach our children without realizing it. "The Tale of the Ungrateful Son" begins with a description of an old merchant who day by day grows more infirm. The old man's wife has long since died, and he is miserably lonely. Fearing that he would soon lose his powers of mind, the old man decides to ask his middle-aged son and daughter-in-law if he might move in with their family.

At first the couple is overjoyed, because the merchant promises to bequeath his small fortune to them before he dies. But the old man in his dotage becomes increasingly troublesome to clean and feed. Eventually his daughter-in-law grows resentful of his constant needs and senile chatter. She harangues her husband night and day, until he reluctantly agrees that the time has come to take the old man to the barn.

The ungrateful son is too embarrassed, however, to confront his father directly with his shameful decision. He gives that chore to his own youngest child.

"Take your grandfather to the barn and wrap him in the best horse blanket we have on the farm," he tells the boy. "That way the old man will be as comfortable as possible until he dies."

With tears in his eyes the child does as he is told, except that, having selected the farm's best horse blanket, he tears it in half. He uses one part to swaddle his beloved grandfather but sets the other part aside. The merchant's son is furious when he learns what his child has done. "What sort of boy are you who would put his own grandfather out in the barn to freeze with only half a horse blanket?" he shouts.

"But father," the child replies, "I'm saving the other half for you."

The young son has learned a powerful lesson from his father: when you are old, you go out to the barn to die. This is a metaphor of course, but metaphors have a way of translating into behaviors that come back to bite us.

> ### Remember:
> - We create legacy by how we live, not how we die.
> - Children can't fully understand how parents feel.
> - We are as imperfect as our parents.
> - We will be remembered for something.

6 The Dangers of Certainty

Why No One Gets Everything Right

> "Doubt is not a pleasant mental state,
> but certainty is a ridiculous one."
>
> Voltaire

I was nineteen. She was five days old, six pounds of human potential for whom my husband and I were now officially responsible. The baby fit snugly between my fingertips and elbow as we left the hospital. I gazed down at her tiny face peeking through the pale pink blanket. I was terrified. I knew little about life, less about love, nothing about babies.

How will I know what each cry means or if she's hungry, or hurts, or is just exercising her lungs? What if I diaper her wrong and the safety pin opens, or she can't breathe in her crib, or the bath water is too cool or my milk won't flow or she won't stop crying?

At home, we lay the baby on the bed, the same bed

where she had been conceived. I cried, more from my overwhelming feeling of responsibility than from joy. I promised her I would be a good mother. I had no idea what that meant.

Her father unwrapped the blanket. Her tiny arms and legs reached upward. He assured me that we would know what to do, that we weren't the first parents who didn't know anything about babies. Bravado, of course. He knew less about babies than I did.

We had created a new life, a new person , knowing little or nothing about how to raise her and have her thrive. Somehow, she did, followed by her sisters, each coded with what we know today are a set of genetic markers cascading from hundreds of generations who preceded us.

Each of those previous generations had coped as we had, with childhood conditioning shaping how we viewed the world. Guided by our own nature and nurture, we continue to bring to parenting a vast subterranean minefield of emotions, abilities, and limitations coded into our DNA.

In addition to our biological heritage, we are part of the fabric of cultural imperatives. Rules, roles, systems, expectations, and assumptions – they all play into the scenario of parenting. Babies are supposed to transform us, guiding us in how to nurture, love and sacrifice for this new life we created.

At least, that's the expectation. What few of us factor into our plans for our babies are the elements we can't control. Genetics and environment are counterbalanced by intentions, hopes and dreams. It's only in retrospect that we can see the detours and forks in the road, that were unpredictable at the time, but forced us to choose a direction.

Who Are We?

We may not like to think that the potential of each child is already contained within that baby blanket. But any parent of more than one child will tell you - babies come into the world, into the same family, with distinct personalities.

The science journal *Nature* headlined a story in 2008 about personal genomics, the emerging science of behavioral genetics that probes the links between genetic coding, brain chemistry and environment. Research scientists are showing that our genetic coding contains not only information about ancestry and heritable diseases, but also clues to our temperaments and abilities, vulnerabilities and choices in life.

Based on what these scientists are learning, the phrase 'runs in the family' may soon be backed up by science, thus rendering the question 'Who am I?' a moot point. A look at our personal genome profile may eventually yield the answers to what made us what we are. Until then, we have to settle for the possibility that we are shaped by our genetic inheritance in ways that none of us can directly know. If we raise our baby with environmental factors that match its coding, our experience of parenting will be different from when coding and environment work against each other

Our expectations for ourselves as parents abound - I'll be a perfect parent. I won't make the same mistakes my parents made. I'll treat my children equally. I'll be fair. I'll be patient, loving, thoughtful, sensitive, supportive, and involved. Their needs will come first. I'll sacrifice for them, keep them from harm...and so forth.

You name it – if it's good, we want it for our children. If it's bad, we intend to keep it away. We mean it, all of it...and we inevitably fall short. Yet have we failed?

To serve as a parent is, for some of us, to have a resume that doesn't match our skills. We have to learn 'on the job' what others with different genetic coding and life experience may do naturally. We are, generation after generation, locked into the interplay of DNA markers, uncontrollable distribution and unpredictable environment.

It's a testament to the power of love that most parents do as well as they do. Think of it ... a baby is born with the DNA coding, tendencies and temperaments of two parents, four grandparents and generations of recombinant DNA lines that preceded them.

This raises some questions. For example, how many of our genetic inclinations matched our environment? Were we predisposed emotionally for parenting? How much resilience did we develop in the aftermath of tragedies, challenges and obstacles many of us faced growing up? How did all of that affect us as parents?

None of us knows what made us what we are. We have stories about our life, but no proof. We've reached conclusions about people and events based on a narrow band of experience. Brain science research is showing that we can be certain of nothing.

Are You Sure?

How do we become certain that something happened the way we think it did and for the reasons we believe?

Robert Burton,M.D, a neurologist who writes about the paradoxical relationship between our thoughts and what we actually know, claims that we can never be certain about anything. His book *On Being Certain: Believing You are Right When You're Not* explores why people trust their 'feeling of knowing' even when presented with evidence to the contrary.

He cites the Challenger explosion in 1986, and the study that was done of 106 college students who were asked the following day to write down exactly how they'd heard about the explosion: where they were, what they'd been doing and how they felt. They were interviewed again two and a half years later. Twenty five percent of the students' subsequent accounts were strikingly different than their original journal entries. Even when presented with their original assessments, the students were certain that their most recent statement was correct.

Because of how our brain operates, new information filters through the neuronal pathways of what is already laid down. In other words, it's hard to see things accurately because our filter only lets through what we expect to see.

Burton writes that any idea that either hasn't been, or isn't capable of being, independently tested should be considered a personal version of reality.

"We cannot say unequivocally that we know something to be true; all we can say is we believe it is so. That leaves room for doubt and further exploration," he writes. "Modern biology tells us that despite how certainty feels, it is neither a conscious choice nor even a thought process. Certainty and similar states of 'knowing what we know' arise out of primary brain mechanisms that, like love or anger, function independently of rationality or reason."

There's no doubt that some parents can and do act monstrously towards their children, robbing them of their childhood and damaging them for life through incest, physical and emotional abuse, abandonment and other acts of horror. The media are filled with heart-rending accounts of parental abuse and a justice system

77

that inadequately metes out justice to abusive parents. Their children often grow up scarred and wounded, and frequently inflict the same abusive behavior on their own children.

I believe that no parent sets out to intentionally hurt or cause his or her children pain, anger, disappointment or hardship. To be a parent is, by definition, to be flawed – well-intentioned perhaps, but most often uninformed and unprepared for this new role. Given what we're learning about genetics, the ability to parent well may, biologically speaking, have its mechanism for failure built in.

Most parents try to give their children the best of themselves, to instill in them their values and enable them to make their way in the world without the need to rely on them. By the same token, they readily admit to lapses of judgment, insensitive and selfish behavior, impatience and a host of other human frailties.

This has important implications for the relationship between parents and children. Is what a child or parent remembers about any situation an accurate account, or a 'feeling of knowing?' If that memory, often based on a misunderstanding, translates into a sense of certainty, it can provide the basis for a belief system that ultimately affects everyone in the family.

"Feeling correct or certain isn't a deliberate conclusion or conscious choice. It is a mental sensation that happens to us, partly determined by our expectations," Burton writes.

You can see this phenomenon at work in autobiographies and memoirs, written by authors convinced that the story they tell is the truth. In their mind, it may be real, but did it actually happen the way they remember?

For example, Joan Crawford, the legendary movie star, will be remembered as much for her daughter's poisonous memoir about her as for her powerful presence onscreen. There is no way to attest to the things described in *Mommie Dearest*. The narrative stands on its own because there is no way to prove or disprove any of it.

Consider what happened to Bette Davis. She suffered a broken hip, a mastectomy, and a series of strokes just before the publication of a scathing and bitter memoir by her daughter B.D. Hyman. A groundswell of public sympathy for Davis caused her friends and other celebrities to come forward. They disputed her daughter's version of events, stating that far from being emotionally abusive, Davis had doted on her daughter. Even 60 Minutes got involved in the controversy by re-running an interview with Hyman, in which she praised her mother's abilities as a parent.

Davis' only public response to her daughter's allegations was a letter she published in her last book, *This 'N That*, written in 1987. She wrote:

"Dear Hyman, I am now utterly confused as to who you are or what your way of life is. Your book is a glaring lack of loyalty and thanks for the very privileged life I feel you have been given. If my memory serves me right, I've been your keeper all these many years. I am continuing to do so, as my name has made your book about me a success."

A previously loving relationship, whether that of lovers, parents, siblings, mentors, or any other where love has been replaced by pain, disillusion, betrayal or disappointment, can activate a need for the 'wronged' person to tell their version of the tale.

These accounts, which I call the 'retributive justice' genre, are penned for different reasons. Telling 'what she really did to me' mitigates or avenges the injustices in the writer's mind. Perhaps the written account solidifies the memory and gives it greater authenticity.

What we don't find are memoirs written by parents about a child. They may write about a child's illness, or accident or other tragedy, often wishing to memorialize their child or help other parents dealing with similar situations. But the "Baby Dearest" memoir has yet to be written.

We would do well to heed Robert Burton's advice: "Hearing myself saying 'I believe,' where formerly I would have said 'I know,' serves as a constant reminder of the limits of knowledge and objectivity. At the same time as I am forced to consider the possibility that contrary opinions might have a grain of truth, I am provided with the perfect rebuttal for those who claim that they 'know that they are right.'"

My Memories, Myself

Memory is an unreliable historian: This is the reason that eyewitness testimony, while allowed in court, is not considered to be reliable evidence. Psychologists tell us that we remember what we pay attention to, ruminating on our impressions and 'making adjustments.' Much of this work happens unconsciously. We then 'remember' events with the modifications.

For example, Laura believed her whole life that her parents loved her younger sister Lila more than her. Three years apart in age, Lila adored her older sister. No matter what their parents did to treat the girls equally, Laura found a detail in every situation to confirm her point of view. For her parents, it was frustrating and often heartbreaking.

It wasn't until years later that Laura's parents learned why she felt that way. Laura had her tonsils out at the age of five, at a time when hospitals didn't allow parents to stay overnight with their child. Laura was in pain; she felt abandoned and frightened. She didn't understand that her parents *couldn't* stay with her. All she knew was that they were going home to take care of Lila.

Laura's parents realized this one incident had laid the foundation stone for her certainty that her parents loved her sister more. The sisters are still not close. The parents are still hurting.

Misunderstandings grow to epic proportions because of an action or reaction we don't understand. Many times, we don't learn what it was that created the misunderstanding in the first place. Sometimes we learn about it decades later and are stunned that something that rolled off us made such an impression on our child.

The potential for mistakes lurks everywhere. When I was a young parent, I made many 'mistakes.' How could I not? I knew little to nothing about parenting and was flying blind. The mistakes weren't necessarily based on misunderstanding something, but on making a decision that turned out to be unwise.

Today, I can't remember many of those decisions, but the evidence of their existence lives on in the memories of my children. They didn't know I was making mistakes. I didn't know I was making mistakes. For them, it was just what I was doing. From this they formed their impression of who I am in relationship to them. Thus, the early development of misunderstandings can last for years.

Many parents, myself included, feel guilt about things we don't remember happening, but which our children claim is true. For example, haven't we all learned years later of some injustice a child remembers, that we don't? The child is certain; we have no content or context for the basis of the story, while the child's whole identity is based on his surety that his story is accurate. Yet he can be, and often is, wrong.

I vaguely remember punishing one of my daughters for something she protested that she had not done. I didn't believe her, and grounded her for a week. I later learned that she hadn't done it, and apologized. She forgave me, but always remembered my rush to judgement.

There are people who can tell you in painstaking detail every hurtful event they 'remember' from their childhood. Ask their sibling about these same events and you will hear a different story. We all do it. Once we have narrative, we shape our memories around the theme. Facts that don't fit we discard, choosing the information to strengthen what we already believe we know. Sometimes we go as far as 'I believe it, therefore I see it.'

If I had understood this earlier, my experience with my own parents, told in the next chapter, would have been different. The same is true for my children and yours. We are blind to our own motives and natures.

One More Psychological Hurdle

Further complicating the nexus of memory and certainty is our human tendency to justify our actions, especially when we know we've made a mistake. Psychologists call the reason for this justification *cognitive dissonance*. Simply stated, it refers to an uneasy state of mind in which a person tries to maintain two contradicting ideas at the same time.

Here's how it works: Our brain is wired for self-justification. When we make mistakes, we are driven to reduce the cognitive dissonance that jars our feelings of self-worth. And so we create fictions that absolve us of responsibility, restoring our belief that we are smart, moral, and right — a belief that often keeps us on a course that is dumb, immoral, and wrong.

For example, a father who thinks of himself as a loving and kind parent spanks his child. The father's behavior doesn't match his self-image; he will justify his behavior by reassuring himself that the child 'needed the spanking to learn a lesson' and that the pain was for the child's own good. Or the person who thinks of herself as loyal shares a secret about her best friend with other women during a night out. Her justification? 'They would find out anyway.' The family man struggling to pay the bills buys a giant TV screen. 'Sure I'll watch the game, but the whole family will enjoy this.'

We evade responsibility when things fall apart, don't own up when we mess things up, argue endlessly about who is right and are very good at seeing the hypocrisy in others, but not in ourselves. Politicians may be an obvious example, but cognitive dissonance exists everywhere. We make promises we don't keep and justify why. We let friends down and have rational reasons for our behavior.

Mistakes Were Made (but not by me) is the title of a book by Carol Travis and Elliot Aronson. The authors provide numerous examples of how our memories, our narratives about ourselves, are built up over the years, shaping an account of how we came to be the way we are. They write, "Memories create our stories, but our stories also create our memories. Once we have a narrative, we shape our memories to fit into it."

Misunderstandings harden into positions. Cognitive dissonance reinforces them. Family relationships disintegrate because parents and children are certain about what they 'know.'

It's appropriate to regret some of the unwise decisions we make. If we knew then what we know now, we might have chosen otherwise. One of life's most difficult tasks is to balance this paradox of our own opposing views, and deal with the cognitive dissonance that results. Perhaps F. Scott Fitzgerald described it best: "The test of a first rate intelligence is the ability to hold two opposed ideas in the mind at the same time and still retain the ability to function." That might even be a definition for mental health.

Remember

- Memory and certainty are incompatible.
- When you are certain, you may be wrong.
- An autobiography is one person's experience.
- Inside every parent lives the child they once were.

7 Death and Rebirth

Recovering from Emotional Wounds

> "Forgive them Lord,
> for they know not what they do."
>
> Jesus Christ

I had always felt and believed that my parents loved me. That's why it was such a devastating blow when my father chose his religion over me. It took many years and a great deal of work, but I healed from the pain of that wound, though its memory remains. What I learned in this work, and the tools I used in the healing process, constitute the remaining chapters of this book.

Death

In retrospect, I could have lied. What's so terrible about lying when it's in the service of a greater good?

And what is the greater good? Who is to judge? And what are their criteria? And what if the reason for the 'good' lie backfires, and buries everyone in its wake? What is the price you pay for a relationship built on a lie?

I could have said, "Yes, Papa, the man I love is Jewish." That would have been enough for him. He would have asked no further questions about ethics, values, politics, profession, or integrity. For my father, those qualities were incidental to Jewish ancestry. To me, being Jewish was not synonymous with being a good person. I didn't lie. It was a dreadful decision.

"Never speak to me again. Or to your mother. Do not call. Do not write. Do not come. You are dead," my father said when I told him about the man I loved. My mother went along.

Nothing in my value system or experience could validate, or even consider, declaring a child dead. For my father, there was nothing in his value system that was worse than marrying out of the faith. Living in America for 30 years had done nothing to mitigate his fervent belief that interfaith marriage is wrong, and that it constitutes the death of the next generation. What was even worse for me was that they knew, and presumably loved, their granddaughters. To declare me dead was to do the same to my children. To choose my parents, I would have had to lie about the man I loved or give him up.

For years I called my parents. I wrote. I knocked on their door. I pleaded. When my father died, no one knew where to reach me. I lived on the West Coast; they lived in New York. My parents had removed me from their address records. Trying once again because I missed my mother so badly, I sent her a birthday card. A cousin who was helping her after my father's death saw the return address and contacted me. I went to be with my mother. She had slipped into senility. She did not acknowledge me. Perhaps she didn't recognize me.

My mother couldn't stay in her apartment, the same apartment where I grew up. We arranged for her to live in a nursing home. My cousin and I packed her possessions. As we went through drawers and closets, there was no sign that I or my daughters had ever lived. All photographs were gone. No names or addresses in their phone book. Every gift my children or I had given to them over the years – gone. Not a trace of us remained. They had wiped us out of their existence.

This is the destructive power of certainty, of believing oneself right and being willing to forsake all connection to people who don't agree with you. My daughters from my first marriage grew up knowing their grandparents were 'strange,' but they always treated them with respect and affection. Here, in one sweeping act of parental tyranny, my children and I were cast out, obliterated by parents and grandparents who declared us officially dead.

For my father to declare us dead served his ego; for my mother, it must have been torturous. When he died, senility was her only safe haven. She lived for five more years in a nursing home. I visited as often as I could, frequently with my husband, whose hand she liked to hold, telling me all the while what a kind and handsome man he is. She never knew who he was, or recognized me again. She died a few years later.

Rebirth

Understanding is not forgiveness. That didn't happen until a few years later, when I had the following dream. By that time, both of my parents had died.

The wooden stairway was narrow, with barely enough room for me to hold onto the banister. The walls on each side of the stairway seemed to be transparent, yet try as I might, I couldn't see anything through them. My eyes were riveted on the door at the top of the stairs. Though I continued to climb, stopping occasionally to catch my breath, I didn't feel I was making any progress. The door appeared to stay the same distance from me no matter how many steps I climbed.

Suddenly, I broke through what felt like a wall of energy. I took the steps two at a time and in a second, held the doorknob in my hand. Standing one-step down from the threshold, I opened the door. I saw a vast expanse of blue sky and a figure walking towards me. It was my father. He approached me, and stepped down onto the step upon which I was standing. A tear rolled down his cheek as he put his arms around me and hugged me tight. "I've been waiting for you," he said.

I awoke and realized I had moved into a new emotional space. I felt my father in the room with me. The tears that fell from my eyes were my father's tears. I felt his pain, his helplessness, and his anger. I experienced his futility, his sense of betrayal, and his battle with his own convictions. Yet in my dream, I had seen the look in his eyes as he approached me. Clearly, it was love that I saw, love that made me weep.

Staying with the feeling, I allowed myself to see his world as he would have seen it.

His only daughter marrying a non-Jew. An abomination. How could she do this to him? To her mother? What was she thinking? That they would just say fine? That it was a choice to marry outside of the religion? To be confronted with what felt like death anyway? What had he done to deserve this? It was like a knife in the heart, and his daughter had driven it in. Better to close the chapter and try to let the scars heal than to be confronted always with her decision. Let everyone think he didn't care. Let them think him crazy. Didn't anyone care about what was important to him? And what was she doing to the grandchildren? She had no right. She had no right. And yet, he loved her. Love doesn't die so easily, even if it hurts you and you are half dead anyway because of the pain. And where to put that love? How to explain to her mother who was suffering more than he with the consequences of his decision? Her mother and he had never had a close or intimate moment again. She had accepted his decision and by her behavior toward him, had also declared him dead.

As these thoughts raced through me, and the tears wouldn't stop, I remembered something I had heard a long time ago - 'Forgiveness is an emotion that happens in an instant.' It had made no sense to me when I heard it. How does one move from agony to forgiveness just like that?

But my emotions did shift, 'just like that.' I felt an overwhelming sense of compassion, a surge of tenderness and commiseration for what must have been one of my parents' most dreadful moments in life. The action, for which there was no excuse, at least had a context which defined it. I didn't agree. I didn't condone. I'll never forget. What I did was to place the pain in context, see things from the other side, and understand how, given who my parents were - what they had experienced as Holocaust survivors, and what their values were - they were acting in complete accord with what they believed.

The View from the Other Side

Students who train to be part of a debating team practice an exercise that requires them to defend their opponent's point of view. Whatever the position they are defending, when the moderator says switch, they must take the opposite point of view and defend it.

It's interesting to note that most of us can do this fairly well, even if we're not training for a debating team. We can do it because we're not emotionally invested in the outcome. However, when it comes to holding a grudge, or an unwillingness to let go of a hurt, we believe it's not possible. But that's not true. It's not only possible to see things from the other person's point of view; it can save a relationship (or at the very least, neutralize the pain).

I wish I had understood this process before my parents died. I would have handled myself differently, allowing myself to see things from their point of view. I would have been intent on finding a way to make things work for all of us, rather than concentrating on the pain I felt because they were not honoring my choice.

There's no guarantee that the outcome would have

been more satisfactory for anyone. What would have been different is that I would have known personally that I had tried whatever I could to restore balance and peace to the situation.

Deconstructing an Emotional Wound

The deconstruction process is a way of standing in another person's shoes and seeing the world through their eyes. It is a useful tool in preventing a rift from occurring in the first place and especially beneficial in helping to heal an emotional wound that was inflicted years before.

The deconstruction process consists of a series of questions. I learned variations of this process at workshops on communication and resolving conflicts. I distilled the process into five steps, which I realized were at the heart of most misinterpretations and subsequent grudges.

These steps include: the situation, the response, the misinterpretation, the conclusion and the resolution. Each step is a building block towards the next. Together and in sequence, they are useful in helping to clarify your motives in having, or maintaining, any misunderstanding.

I use my experience with my father to illustrate the process in the example that follows. The questions used in this process are repeated at the end of the chapter (without my responses), so you can use them for yourself.

The Deconstruction Process

Describe the situation from your point of view.
I was in love with a man who wasn't Jewish. It was

a second marriage for both of us. We were both adults. I wanted my parents to meet him because I believed they would see he was a good man and they would like him.

Describe the situation from their point of view.
They believed that by rejecting their faith, I was rejecting them. They had been raised with the belief that intermarriage was against Jewish law. They lived in a Jewish neighborhood. They believed that their friends and family would be horrified that I had married out of the faith. They felt humiliated, and didn't understand that the world outside of their insular view didn't perceive intermarriage as the grievous act they considered it to be.

What precisely did they not understand?
They didn't understand that independent adults have a right to choose whom they will marry. They didn't understand that I didn't want to lie, and I didn't want to have to choose between them and the man I loved.

Why do you think they could not understand?
They could not understand because of their belief that marrying out of the faith is an act against God, and an insult to what they had sacrificed for their faith during the Holocaust.

What did I not understand?
I didn't understand how deeply rooted their faith was. I didn't understand how ashamed they would feel in the family that their daughter had made this choice. I didn't understand how narrow minded my father was despite three decades in America. I didn't understand that my mother would stand by

my father's decision.

How did you explain yourself?
I tried to reason with my father, saying that if he met my future husband, he would like him. That he was a good man, kind to my daughter and to me, had a business and that he would make a good life with us.

Did your explanation make sense to them?
No. My parents were angry and hurt. The only thing they responded to was the difference in religion. They saw this as an 'us or him' situation.

Did they ask you the same questions over again?
Yes. They asked, "How can you do this to us?"

Was your explanation satisfactory to you at the time?
At first it was. I soon realized that I had made a mistake.

How did they react when they couldn't or didn't understand?
They told me they never wanted to see my children or me again. They wanted me to stay away from the rest of the family.

If you could explain yourself today, what would you say?
I would say I was sorry for having offended them by my choice. I would ask what they suggest I do, instead of maintaining my right to do what I pleased as an adult.

Would your explanation move you closer to resolution?
I don't know. The outcome may have been the same unless I chose them over the man I loved.

Are you willing to let the other person be right?
In this case, there doesn't seem to be right or wrong. Choosing my parents would have allowed my children and me to continue our relationships with them, instead of losing them. I could have waited to marry my husband after they got to know him in a social setting. In retrospect, I could have lied and said that my husband is Jewish. He would have been able to carry it off. We both could have chosen to lie.

Philosophically, lying is a slippery slope and I try not to do it. However, there are some instances when lying seems like the kind thing to do. If I had thought more deeply about my parents' response, rather than my preference for their response, I would have realized that the truth was something they could not live with. I had to shoulder my responsibility in triggering their response, even though I could never fathom it.

Let's summarize the five steps in the deconstruction process: the situation, the response, the misinterpretation, the conclusion and the resolution.

These five steps in deconstructing my emotional pain and switching to their point of view helped me realize that, horrible as it was, I was a participant in the outcome. I couldn't change the result, or perhaps I wouldn't change it. Perhaps I preferred maintaining my position instead of compromising towards a resolution. But it helped for me to realize that I had a choice and I made it. That's exactly how my parents felt.

Use this process for your own emotional healing; the steps are repeated in the box on the facing page.

Deconstructing an Emotional Wound

Describe the situation from your point of view

Describe the situation from their point of view

What precisely did the other person not understand?

Why do you think they could not understand?

What did you not understand?

How did you explain yourself?

Did your explanation make sense to them?

Did they ask you the same question over again?

Was your explanation satisfactory to you at the time?

How did they react when they couldn't or didn't understand?

If you could explain yourself today, what would you say?

Would your explanation move you closer to resolution?

Are you willing to let the other person be right?

When you finish this process, you should be closer to answering some key questions about your role in any misunderstanding. You will also learn more about how your own heart and mind work.

It's an odd thing about forgiveness. We can't control whether or not a person will forgive us. We can only deal with our own desire, and ability, to forgive. It takes two people to structure a hurt, but only one to let it go. This is compassion and I believe it is at the heart of forgiveness. Compassion and anger can't occupy the same space at the same time.

Remember:

- Stand in someone else's shoes and the world changes.

- Holding a grudge is a choice to be in pain.

- Attachment to an outcome interferes with resolution.

8 The Power to Forgive

How Language Shapes Forgiveness

> *"Resentment is like drinking poison, and waiting for it to kill your enemy."*
>
> Nelson Mandela

We've been taught to think of forgiveness as a gift we bestow on another. In reality, forgiveness is a gift we give to ourselves. It doesn't matter if the other person knows about it or not. It's a self-affirming realization that we can shed a burden we've been carrying. We don't have to forget, condone or excuse. What we're doing when we forgive is *separating the pain from the memory*. It enriches our life because we know more clearly who we are and who others are – and how we will relate to them in the future.

I've experienced forgiveness as a sensation that swept over me in an instant. It didn't feel like a choice;

it just showed up as an awareness that a burden had been lifted. The process of working towards forgiveness wasn't easy, but it would have been easier if I had understood it better at the time.

Forgiveness only requires one person – you. That holds true whether you are the parent who wants to forgive a child or a child who wants to forgive your parent. Let's take a closer look at how this works.

Everybody makes mistakes. I've made many. Some have hurt only me; others have hurt people I care about. When I knew I had hurt someone, I apologized. If I did not know that I hurt them and they didn't tell me, I often watched a friendship or other relationship end.

When I asked if I had done anything to hurt them, I was often told, "You know what you did." Truthfully, sometimes I did know, but had let my ego justify my behavior because I wouldn't admit I was wrong. Other times I didn't know, but wanted to restore a friendship or relationship. I was surprised by how often people would not tell me what the problem was.

None of us gets it right all the time. Our life is a series of lessons from which we learn and grow. We feel guilty for things we have done; we feel resentment and anger for things others have done. The blame and shame cycle never ends until we understand that we can do something about it. We can't change what already happened. However, we can seek to understand, try to fix it through apology and forgiveness, and ultimately move on.

For example, Wanda had been looking after her daughter's dog when the dog unexpectedly died. Wanda's grief was compounded by the guilt and remorse she felt. Five years later, she was still blaming herself as if it happened last week. Holding on to her blame and guilt couldn't bring the dog back. Wanda needs to forgive herself.

Judy's daughter still reminds her of all the times, as a child, she felt abandoned when her mother traveled. Now that she is raising her own children, she won't leave them with a sitter, pointing out to Judy that she doesn't want her kids to feel abandoned as she did.

Examples of hurt, neglect, pain are endless, but they share some characteristics when it comes to the need for forgiving others and forgiving ourselves.

Consider this: we are not the same people we were when we experienced the problem. We aren't even the same person we were yesterday, let alone a day, a month or a year ago. On the other hand, everything that happened to us is, like an airplane's black box, logged in whether we're aware of it or not. No matter how hard we try, we don't forget. What we can change, however, is how we deal with what happened. *Forgiveness accepts the actuality of what happened.*

Unfortunately, the same assumptions and misunderstandings that occur between lovers or spouses can happen between parents and children. Unrealistic expectations about how relationships are 'supposed' to function can lead to years of mutually hardened positions.

Run out the scenarios yourself by finishing the sentences: "If my husband really loved me, he'd know ..." "If Mom really loves me, she would..." or "How can my father say he loves me when he..." These one-sided emotional demands require another person to read our mind, know what we want, know when we're hurt and understand what they need to do to fix the relationship.

Hurt feelings build on themselves. Grudges accumulate, resentment hardens until a relationship is transformed by the bitterness that one person may feel without the other understanding why.

Instead of saying, "You hurt my feelings, I don't understand why you said that" or "Let's talk about what happened," or "I may owe you an apology for something I said but don't understand why it hurt you," we slam the door on the relationship. We claim that the other person, 'if they really loved us,' should have known better.

What a tall order to ask of other people. This kind of thinking has happened to me in my family. Perhaps it's happened in yours. Often you'll learn about something that happened decades earlier that hurt someone's feelings. In all that time, you've changed and grown but you're still viewed through the filter of an event or remark from the past.

I don't include acts that are heinous and unforgivable such as incest, rape, and physical abuse. There are no extenuating circumstances, no context, no justification for these. Some humans act despicably and their actions scar people for life.

Throughout this book, I've stressed the ordinary garden variety of insensitive, thoughtless, selfish, and often unintentional words or actions that can sever family relationships for years. I've described how our perception of reality often becomes reality, because of how our minds work.

Why People Won't Forgive

We repeat behaviors because we receive a benefit from them; if there were no benefit, we would change the behavior. Although it seems illogical, we often gain from holding on to a grievance or grudge. Like a sore tooth to which the tongue returns again and again to probe the pain, we treat grudges like prized possessions, pulling them out to review, ruminate and reinforce the negative and often painful feelings we experienced from words or events, that occurred sometimes decades before.

What benefit can there be from this kind of behavior? Consider the following possibilities.

Some people like playing the victim. Suffering is a state that excuses a lot of other behavior such as procrastination, lack of achievement, poor health, and a host of personal failures they can blame on someone.

People have an ego investment in not forgiving one another. Remember our previous discussion of cognitive dissonance and how we guard our point of view? When our self-image is at stake, we often fight to the finish rather than admitting that something may be our fault. We do it as individuals and as nations.

Sometimes, the unwillingness to forgive is a power play, an attempt to foster guilty feelings about something without allowing for its correction. Sometimes, it's an excuse to end a relationship we no longer find satisfying. Or, it could be a fear that, if we forgive, we're letting that person off-the-hook for their behavior.

The person who won't forgive us when we ask for it has a reason for hanging on to the grievance. We can't change that person's mind; we can only change our own.

The Anatomy of Apology

One of the most mindless phrases that ever came into widespread use is from the 1970 movie "Love Story." Ryan O'Neal and Ali McGraw play two young lovers torn apart by cancer and untimely death. "Love means never having to say you are sorry," murmurs Ali as she edges toward her final moments.

Wrong, Ali. Love not only allows you to say you're

sorry, but *requires* that you do - not an offhand 'I'm sorry about that,' but a *real* apology, built on a truthful and thorough acknowledgement of the offense (and its subsequent effect on the injured party). There's no room for blame-sharing in a true apology ('I'm sorry but...' or 'I did it because you...'), nor can it be said in anger. The sincerity of a real apology stems from the remorseful party following a series of intentional steps; recognizing, taking responsibility, regretting, renouncing and reconciling.

We can't demand an apology from someone else. It's either freely offered or its authenticity and sincerity is compromised. The only apology we can extend is our own. The important thing to remember is that we have the power to forgive others, whether they forgive us or not. If our objective is to heal a relationship, to reconcile, apologizing is the first step. To add a lighter touch here, let's credit that famous wordsmith Anonymous who reminds us that 'an apology is a good way to have the last word.'

Recognition and Responsibility

First, we have to be aware, that what we have done has hurt someone. We may have broken a promise or neglected someone we love. It might be something we did or didn't do. We can't recognize this unless we slow down and pay attention to how our relationship with a loved one is flowing. Slowing down, paying attention, being present are important first steps. If a relationship feels as if it's off track for us, it often feels that way for the other person too. If you feel there might be something off in your relationship, ask. Be willing to find out that someone has a problem with you.

Once we realize we have neglected, offended, forgotten something important, or whatever it is that's the problem, we need to discern if we feel sorry. If so, and only if so, we need to take ownership of our part, our language, and our participation. We need to refer to the event or words that caused the hurt. We need to say, "I apologize for..." Being specific is what makes the apology sincere.

If someone responds with a sweeping generalization by saying 'You always...' or 'You never...,' or keeps reiterating their evaluation of why you did it and who you are, that's a sign that the other person isn't hearing your apology.

Basically, taking responsibility means acknowledging ownership of the event or situation in which we caused pain to someone. To be sorry is not to be weak or wrong. Instead, it shows strength of character, because it testifies to our admission that we are a participant in a situation, and could have chosen to act otherwise. Remember, the language of responsibility is 'I'm sorry,' not 'I regret.'

Regret and Remorse

Regret is impersonal, concerned with consequences rather than feelings. Expressing regret means that if we had a chance to do it again, we'd probably do it differently only because we know the outcome. Politicians, corporations, and governments express regrets about many things. They're not saying they regret their actions; they only regret the outcome.

I remember a friend expressing regret when I told her I was hurt that she hadn't invited me to an event in which our other friends were participating. Her response was, "I regret you feel that way." Ouch.

Insincerity runs rampant in public life. Remember

the 'apology' of Senator Tom Delay in front of the Senate Ethics Committee investigating allegations of his financial illegalities?

"I'm apologizing for the conduct that it was alleged that I did," he said smugly, probably hoping no one would find out what he did. His shallow apology was prompted only by the fear of getting caught, not by remorse at his behavior.

Or Mel Gibson apologizing for his anti-Semitic remarks when arrested for drunk driving. The police report records his statement to the arresting officer as, "The Jews are responsible for all the wars in the world. Are you a Jew?" His publicist issued Gibson's apology: "Please know from my heart that I am not an anti-Semite. I am not a bigot. Hatred of any kind goes against my faith."

I've never met a person who doesn't have faults or who hasn't made mistakes. I do know people who will never admit to one. They don't seem to feel remorse, or even regret, about something they did that hurt you, even when you tell them about it. They are typically more interested in defending their actions than restoring a relationship. I believe that when you run into a situation like that, the most loving thing you can do for yourself is recognize that the other person is emotionally handicapped in a profound way.

Remorse is a deep, personal reaction to a hurt we've caused. We are viscerally uncomfortable about what we've done, feeling we've violated our own standards. With remorse, we often feel shame and are forced to question who we are and what our values are.

An important first step for dealing with remorse is self-forgiveness, the process of accepting the inevitability of mistakes by refusing to be defined by them. In fact, successful apologies occur most frequently when we first forgive ourselves for the mistakes we've made. If people we have hurt are prepared to forgive us by accepting the apology and moving past our mistake, the message they're sending is that they value the relationship and respect our character.

> *Remember:*
>   - Forgiveness is a solo act.
>   - Forgiveness is intentional.
>   - Forgiveness is always possible.

9 *Conversations from the Heart*

Guidelines for the Most Important Conversations

> *"The heart has its reasons of which reason knows nothing."*
>
> Blaise Pascal

Each of us is at the mercy of a random event that can pierce the ordinariness of daily life. For example, on holiday weekends, the National Highway Safety Board regularly issues predictions of how many people are expected to die or be seriously injured in a car accident. Yet statistics repeatedly show that most car accidents happen within two miles from home.

On August 20, 2008, Spanair Flight 5022 burst into flames upon take-off, and crashed at the Madrid airport. Spain declared a three-day period of mourning for the 153 victims.

To most of us, the dead are just names. Yet, for each of the victims, a family grieved. An ordinary flight to a vacation destination – what went wrong, how could this happen? A technical explanation of why the plane crashed may quiet the survivor's mind; for the heart, there is no comfort.

I watched the footage of the burning wreckage and all I could think of was how suddenly life can change. People we love die, and the things we mean to say can no longer be said. We never tell them how much we love them, how grateful we are for all they teach and give us, how much we admire them and how lucky we are that they share our life. We wait, thinking we have all the time in the world. We will tell them at the right time, when we aren't so busy, when we figure out what we want to say. Unfortunately, we don't give much thought to the reality: all we have is *this* moment.

Closer to home, what could be more ordinary than kids calling out "We're going to the mall, Mom. See you later."

On December 5, 2007, a suicidal teenager, who had lost his job and his girlfriend, mowed down nine people with a rifle at a mall in Omaha, Nebraska. One shooter, nine grieving families, dozens of lives altered in minutes.

What always races through my mind when I read about events like this is, 'Did the survivors have a chance to say "I love you" before their loved one left for work? Did the people who died know how much they were loved? Were they angry before they left the house? Did the survivors know how much the people who died loved them?'

I wonder whether the survivors would bear, in addition to the pain and grief of their loss, the awareness that they never said the things they could have, if they had known their loved ones would die that day.

Sometimes the random event happens to a trained professional. No one knows why Steve Fossett, a noted aviator and explorer, crashed in his plane in the Nevada desert in September 2007. Rescue teams searched for months with no luck, until two years later when a hiker discovered his identification papers. DNA tests of bones found nearby confirmed Fossett's death.

For a seasoned aviator and explorer like Fossett, who had survived crashes all over the world in planes and balloons and walked away, this short flight was like a trip to the corner grocery store. He was familiar with the route and hadn't bothered to file a flight plan. I thought of his wife and the agonizing wait she endured as searchers combed the area to find him. His last words to her were "I'll be back before lunch." What a cruel irony to die on a clear beautiful morning over an area he knew so well.

In the previous instances, people could not have known that they would never see their loved ones again. However, people are often faced with situations that they know may or will end in death. Some talk about what could happen and others don't. I think families are better served by being realistic, expressing their fears and their love.

If you have the chance and you don't take it, you're setting yourself up for additional pain and regret if someone close to you dies.

Roger, the husband of my friend Diana, required serious heart surgery. They knew the risks involved and prepared for the worst, making sure their financial and legal documents were up–to-date. Just as important, they didn't close down their feelings about what they had meant to each other, and the life they had built together, over three decades of marriage.

The surgery was scheduled for two weeks in advance. Asking their four children to visit earlier, rather than gathering on the day of the surgery, the family spent days poring over photo albums and home movies, remembering happy times and sharing feelings about what they mean to each other. Tom, the youngest child, who had been estranged from the family for years, didn't show up.

Roger spent time alone with each of the three children who came, wanting to be sure they had the chance to say to him what was personal to them. He wanted to give each their own blessing and tell them individually that he loved them.

At the time of this writing, Roger is recovering, but he will need additional surgery. He would still like to talk with Tom, but this may not happen. Tom may find himself in a 'race-to-the-bedside' situation. On the other hand, he may not care. But consider what Roger has given to his family, because he was willing to have those conversations from the heart.

Anne's mother is 89 years old, still lucid, still driving, still living in her two story house, refusing to spend money to make the house safer for someone who lives alone. Anne and her sister Audrey live nearby and Mom wants them to do things for her. The sisters are gradually being worn down, because Mom refuses to cooperate in making the situation easier for anyone. The sisters feel resentful; every discussion with their mother about practical matters ends with anger or frustration. Money is not the issue here; it is the mother's desire for continued control.

The sisters are in a bind; let their mom fend for herself, and they will worry and feel guilty. Continue to interact with their mother this way, and each of them will suffer. The mother gets to have things exactly the way she wants them.

They finally broke the impasse by stressing the principles we'll discuss below. They told their mother how much they love her, how grateful they are for everything she's done for them, how much they care about her and want her to be safe, and how much they have learned from her.

After this lead in, they explained what they *were* and *were not* willing to continue to do for her, and then they gave her some choices.

Mom could interview housekeepers *or* they could do it for her. She could hire a gardener *or* they could find one for her. She could order her groceries and have them delivered *or* wait until her daughters were going shopping. She could sell the car through a dealer *or* they could place an ad for her in the local paper. She could take a taxi to visit her friends *or* they could drive her if they had some notice.

You get the idea... What they began to do was provide Mom with choices, so she didn't feel they were trying to run her life. But Anne and Audrey's choices reflected newly-established boundaries, thereby easing their resentment. It would have been different if Mom couldn't make decisions due to dementia or Alzheimer's disease - in that case, the sisters would have had to make those decisions.

Guidelines for Crucial Conversations

There are two kinds of crucial conversations. The objective of the first is practical information – what do parents need to share with children so the children can help them when needed as they age. This information includes legal, financial, medical, social, and end-of-life preferences (a list of these is included in the appendix of this book).

The second type of conversation has a different goal. It can be more difficult because this is the landscape in which we have invested so much of our self-image – the emotional minefields of misunderstandings, perceptions, expectations, and justifications. The goal of these conversations is to resolve unfinished business - this is the landscape of the heart.

Both kinds of conversation require sensitivity, kindness and respect between parents and children. Whether you are the parent or the adult child who is initiating the conversation, it's easier to open the dialogue if you remember three things.

First, your reality is not their reality. If you let go of demands that the past *should* have been different, because *you* would have acted differently in their shoes, you're well along the path of opening your mind and heart. Don't judge or challenge the other's point of view; instead listen to *really* hear and acknowledge their reality.

Second, the difference between the mindset of a preference and a demand can be the space between heaven and hell. Instead of demanding that a situation be other than it is, you can, if you want to, reframe it as a preference. Reframing uses different language than demanding. For example, the accusation "You didn't come to my graduation..." can be reframed to "I felt very bad when you didn't come to my graduation." It's softer and allows the other person to feel regret or remorse rather than justification of their behavior. The pain occurs in the space between the preference and the demand.

Third, learn to preface all difficult conversations

with at least one of what I call the 'Triple A's: Acknowledgement, Appreciation and Agreement.' You'd be surprised how statements that express all or at least one of these qualities help to soften the listener's heart and allow them to hear what you are saying.

Examples of 'Triple A' sentences (you add your own ending):

I really admire how you...

Have I ever told you how much I appreciate...

I want to thank you for...

One of the things I've always loved about you is...

I can't imagine life without you because...

I've always appreciated the fact that you...

I agree with you about...and I'm concerned about...

Whatever you have to discuss after you allow someone to relax with you will be much easier when you have his or her attention. The best way to get that is to show them they need not feel threatened in any way.

There are a few ways to start these conversations about practical matters. One that is the most effective is the story angle, where something happened that reminded you to speak to your parents or your children about your own concerns. These might include:

I read about a woman who...

I'm really concerned about...

A friend told me about a man who...

At the office, they were talking about...

On one of the money talk shows, this older woman called in...

If you were me, what would you do about...

Remember _____? Someone said she had to sell her house when her husband died. I'm scared that could happen to you Mom...

You're the one who knows your parents/children best, so you can finish the sentences with something personal that makes sense for your relationship. And keep in mind the importance of respect, kindness, and appreciation as precursors to crucial conversations with anyone.

Before You Meet

Send a quick note or email, or make a simple phone call, and mention that there are some things you want to talk about. Ask the other person when would be a good time for them.

Make a checklist of the topics you'd like to discuss and, if appropriate, share it with the other person as the conversation starter – or use this guide as a starting point.

Involve others if possible – parents may want to have these discussions with all of their children together. For children, enlist the support of your siblings if needed.

For children, consider having a preliminary meeting with siblings to get consensus on goals for a meeting with parents. If there is no consensus – which is frequently the case – decide which sibling is most likely to activate the discussion with the least amount of friction.

Begin the conversation casually with your parents or children – ask about their health and well-being, or relate a current event or family health matter that ties into the topics to be discussed.

Don't feel the need to cover all topics in one discussion – it may take a few conversations to cover the various topics.

Record the conversations so you can share them with your siblings. If anyone is uncomfortable with recording, assure them it is for purposes of accuracy because your memory isn't what it used to be. This goes for boomers and seniors. It also allows people to hear the nuances in the conversation that may signal the need for further discussion.

Let the Conversation Unfold

Conversations from the heart work better in a relaxed atmosphere. Don't have this conversation at the holiday table or a family reunion. Don't have this conversation on the phone with either your parents or your children.

Go for a walk or visit a favorite place

Create a relaxing environment, perhaps talking over a cup of coffee or tea

Plan breakfast or lunch at a nearby restaurant

Consider a long drive in the car, a great opportunity to talk without interruption

Make sure any small children are occupied to minimize interruptions

Avoid busy days – like holidays – when many family and friends might be around

Make sure you and the person in the conversation are rested and ready to discuss the issues

A Legacy of Trust and Love

This is the other kind of conversation, the one that deals with unfinished business that can be a huge emotional burden after a parent dies. The same issues can interfere with your ability to open your heart the way you'd like to before it's too late. The guidelines listed above apply here as well. The questions that follow go to the heart of the matter.

As we saw earlier, cognitive dissonance, the conflict between who we *think* we are and how we *actually* behave, keeps us from being open to feedback about how others perceive us. The hardest thing to change is our perception of ourself.

The spirit that drives these conversations from the heart must be reciprocity. You get a chance to listen. You also get the chance to speak. The two-way flow is part of the deal.

In order to listen for comprehension and not let your defenses kick in, you need to swallow your pride, abandon your ego defenses, change your certainty and conquer your fear. You need to see yourself as your child or parent sees you, so you can understand where their perceptions come from. This can be the beginning of wisdom, perhaps even redemption. This may be the best legacy a parent can give a child.

If you're the parent, keep in mind that each of your children had a different experience of you as they were growing up. To honor them individually with time and attention, and encourage a crucial conversation about things you suspect you might have done better, is an act of love. It is something your children may never have anticipated. I guarantee it will move your relationship into a new phase, something you didn't think was possible.

Before You Start

Before you begin this process, keep the following points in mind:

It can be difficult for people to be emotionally open, especially if they have something they have kept to themselves for many years. You need to encourage them with assurances that you want to know; that you're initiating this conversation because you care about what they think and feel and that you want to clear up any misunderstandings or hurt.

Don't get defensive or angry. If you exhibit either of these behaviors, the other person will shut down. This conversation is meant to restore loving feelings, not repeat the emotional pain of previous ones. Remember, the other person's view is true for them. Let them express it without interruption or judgment.

Give the conversation time and privacy. Go someplace where you can be alone without worrying about interruptions.

You might find it useful to list a few things you remember as having caused a problem between you. You may need to begin by writing a letter about these and asking for some time together to clear them up.

Remember: you may be tempted to defend or explain your decisions or actions. Don't do it. If you initiate this conversation, this is a listening session for you. If you want to explain anything someone took in the wrong way, jot a note down and save it for the end of the conversation. Then ask for permission to share that.

If you completed the Deconstruction Process in Chapter 7, you already have an idea of how to put yourself in the other person's shoes. The first five questions on the facing page relate to specific issues or problems between you. The remainder are more general and cover the areas that people who love each other want to say while they still can.

Dr. Ira Byock is a palliative care physician and author of *Dying Well: The Prospect for Growth at the End of Life*. In his work with people nearing the end of their life, he has witnessed the incredible power of four simple sentences: "Please forgive me," "I forgive you," "Thank you," and "I love you." Dr. Byock believes they carry enormous power. In many ways, perhaps they are the most powerful words in any language.

Clean Grief

As I wrote in the introduction, my response to my husband's death and to the death of my parents could not have been more different. I had no unfinished business with my husband. We had many financial challenges and the usual things that married couples deal with. However, the conversations from the heart we had before he died meant that there were no emotional burdens I carried after his death.

Yes, I was devastated by grief and didn't know if I

The Most Important Questions

What could I have done differently?

How did my choice impact you?

What would you have done in my place?

How would that have changed our relationship?

What do you need from me now to move forward?

Do your parents and children know that you love them?

How do you know that they know?

What do you most respect and admire about them?

What is the most important thing you want them to know?

What are you most grateful for?

What makes you proud of your children?

What would you have changed if you could?

Do you need to ask for forgiveness?

would ever feel good again. But I experienced no guilt, no shame, no blame, no resentment. My grief was what I call 'clean.'

That's what I've tried to convey to you in these pages. Conversations from the heart clear the emotional hurdles between you and someone you love. You say what you need to say, with permission from the other person, and in turn, you invite them to say what's in their heart before it's too late. You're leaving each other a legacy of trust and love.

Don't wait to say these things to each other. A 'race-to-the-bedside' could be too late.

Remember:

- You can say anything if your motive is love.
- All the time we have is the space between breaths.
- How will you feel if the person you love dies without these conversations from the heart taking place?

Afterword

Many of you may not have had the chance to clear the emotional channels with people you loved before they died. You will, in essence, be completing the process as I did with my parents, after the fact.

Working alone with the questions and processes in this book can leave you feeling up in the air. I found it useful and effective to create a boundary, a transition space, between my old and new way of thinking and feeling.

Marking this transition with a ritual or symbolic act can add emotional impact to what you've just accomplished. It doesn't have to be part of a religious, family or community tradition .You want something that will be meaningful to you personally. There is no right or wrong way to mark a transition. There is only your way. You can create the legacy of love with the person who died by recognizing your intention.

People who are not religious often find comfort in the simple act of lighting a candle, listening to a favorite piece of music or visiting a beautiful spot in nature. The awareness you bring to what you have accomplished for yourself is your entry into this new territory. It is your gift to yourself.

For my transition, I chose the Jewish prayer for the dead. The Kaddish is a short prayer that, when spoken aloud, is thought to have a spiritual impact on the soul of a departed relative. The prayer leaves a powerful emotional impression on those who say it.

After the dream about my father, I was able to visit my parents' grave for the first time since they died. It was a powerful healing experience for me. I personalized the ritual prayer to reflect the depth of my feelings after so many years.

A Personal Kaddish

Few Jewish daughters have resisted saying Kaddish as long as I have. Somehow, the scripted prayer itself feels incomplete...too universal, too generic, too institutionalized to capture how I'm really feeling. So I'm adding my personal prayer to the traditional Kaddish words which I speak for you for the first time today.

I wonder if your spirits lingered, waiting all these years to hear Kaddish. I am after all, your only daughter. Had you, after all these years of silence, given up hope that you would ever hear the prayer from me? I too had almost given up hope that I could ever say the words. Even in these last few weeks, when I was teaching myself the Hebrew words, I never said them out loud, committing them in silence to memory, carefully safeguarding an escape route near my heart in case I changed my mind.

Today, I have spoken these words that you may have been waiting for. I hope they bring you some comfort for all the agony you experienced as a result of your choices. For me, there is an overwhelming sense of miraculous intervention. I believe God wanted me to take this journey home and honor your memory with forgiveness and love.

So here I stand, at your grave, with appreciation for all the years of caring and concern, for the times of sacrifice, of 'letting the child eat first.' May you rest in peace and love and know that Kaddish will be recited in your memory from this day forth.

Acknowledgements

It is impossible to understand how a book that seems to have lived inside me for years finally comes to life. Many people inspired and encouraged me along the way.

Thanks to Mary Alice Kellogg and Ardy Bazarian who cushioned me through the pain of 'dying.' To Sydney Kapchan, Steve Tulkin , Sherri Rose and Ellen Schwab, thank you for supporting me as forgiveness gave me new life.

Marya Alexander, Susan Gilbert, Jacqui Lopez, Deborah & Stan Jernigan, Sally Pera, Jim Charnes and Julia Michael – your friendship is the wind beneath my wings.

Thanks to my colleagues Denise Hughes and Cathie Orlowski for your encouragement and patience. I thank Paul King, Lloyd Yamada, Peter Johnson, Ann Marshall Robbeloth, Jason Papier, and Craig, Peggy and Hilary Martin. These legal and financial professionals were pivotal in showing me the value of this information when they invited me to speak to their clients about opening these conversations from the heart.

To the people who shared their stories with me, I promised you confidentiality, and I thank you collectively. Your honesty shed light on many of the topics covered in this book.

Many thanks to Lisa Wolfklain for greatly improving my first manuscript, and to Caroline Pincus who guided the final manuscript to completion. Special thanks to Lee Saunders Wright for her penetrating insights and commitment to excellence.

Finally, thank you to my daughters Linda, Julie and Emily, who showed me that imperfect parenting can still result in exceptional offspring.

Suggested Reading

Becker, Ernest. *The Denial of Death*. New York, Free Press Paperbacks, 1973

Bonder, Nilton. *The Kabbalah of Money: Insights on Livelihood, Business, and All Forms of Economic Behavior*. Boston, Shambhala Publications, 1996

Buchan, James. *Frozen Desire: The Meaning of Money*. New York, Farrar, Strauss & Giroux, 1997

Burton, Robert A. MD. *On Being Certain: Believing You are Right Even When You're Not*. New York, St. Martin's Press, 2008

Byock, Ira. MD. *Dying Well: Peace and Possibilities at the End of Life*. New York, Riverhead Books, 1997

Church, Forrest. *Love & Death: My Journey Through the Valley of the Shadow*. Boston, Beacon Press, 2008

Coleman, Joshua. *When Parents Hurt: Compassionate*

Strategies When You and Your Grown Child Don't Get Along. New York, Harper Collins, 2007

Goleman, Daniel. *Vital Lies, Simple Truths; The Psychology of Self-Deception.* New York, Simon and Schuster, 1985

Hendlin, Steven J. *Overcoming the Inheritance Taboo: How to Preserve Relationships and Transfer Possessio.ns.* New York, Penguin Group 2004

Luskin, Frederick, *Forgive for Good: A Proven Prescription for Health and Happiness.* New York, Harper Collins, 2002.

Needleman, Jacob. *Money and the Meaning of Life.* New York, Doubleday, 1991

Oakley, Barbara. *Evil Genes: Why Rome Fell, Hitler Rose, Enron Failed, and My Sister Stole My Mother's Boyfriend.* Amherst, N.Y., Promethus Books, 2008

Pipher, Mary. *Another Country: Navigating the Emotional Terrain of Our Elders.* New York, Riverhead Books, 1999

Scherman, Harry. *The Promises Men Live By: A New Approach to Economics.* New York, Random House, 1938

Scott-Maxwell, Florida. *The Measure of My Days: One Woman's Vivid, Enduring Celebration of Life and Aging.* New York, Alfred A. Knopf, 1968

Tavris, Carol and Aronson, Elliot. *Mistakes Were*

Made (but not by me): Why We Justify Foolish Beliefs, Bad Decisions, and Hurtful Acts. Orlando, FL. Harcourt Books, 2007.

Yalom, Irvin D. *Staring at the Sun: Overcoming the Terror of Death.* San Francisco, Jossey-Bass, 2008

Zelizer, Viviana. *Pricing the Priceless Child: The Social Value of Children.* New Jersey, Princeton University Press, 1994

The Legacy Binder: What Parents Need to
Have & Children Need to Know

O ne of the smartest, most thoughtful and loving thing parents can and should do for their children is keep all their records together. In case of illness, emergency or death, the last thing children should have to deal with is confusion about financial, legal, medical, and end-of-life preferences that they did not know about.

At a time of crisis or grief, the ability to think clearly is severely compromised. It's hard to make decisions about anything. It's even harder to try to find papers and records that could easily, with a little bit of planning and forethought, have been gathered and catalogued in advance. As it represents the final act of love parents can offer their children, I refer to this as the Legacy Binder.

There are commercial binders for this purpose available (such as *Life.Doc* and *Vital Records PortaVault)*, with pre-labeled tabs and document pockets for organizing your records and papers. You can also make your own binder and insert tabbed sheets for each category. The important thing is to have a system that you can easily update if any information changes. For everyone's protection, make sure that any changes are noted and included in the appropriate section in the binder.

Adult children should know where this binder is kept. Under no circumstances should it be stored in a safety deposit box, as loved ones may need access to the information outside of banking hours. If parents don't want to disclose financial information, they should at least have the financial and legal contacts listed in case the children need them. Funeral preferences should be readily available because this is the first thing children will have to deal with.

You can keep the binder in a fireproof safe as long as your family has the combination. If you choose to keep the originals of legal documents in a safety deposit box, be sure adult children are authorized to enter it. If a name is not on a signature card, the contents of the safety deposit box are not available at a time when information inside may be needed.

By assembling all of your critical papers and information in a Legacy Binder, it will be quickly and efficiently available when needed, saving your loved ones the unnecessary burden, and added despair, of being uncertain of your wishes and/or having to search through your files during a period of grief or distress.

What to Put In Your Legacy Binder

Note: All of the information that follows is available, in check-list or fill-in format, on my website (**www.moneylovelegacy.com**). These forms are free of charge, so you can download and print copies to assist you in assembling your binder, and to help insure no documents or planning elements have been overlooked.

Emergency Medical Information

This important emergency medical information - your medical directive and durable power of attorney for health care - needs to be readily available and easy to find, as it is most often needed during a medical crisis when time is limited. If you wish to keep these papers within your Legacy Binder, make sure they are at the front and clearly marked. Remember, these are the documents that will instruct your children, spouse, or loved ones of your wishes in the case of a debilitating accident (or serious deterioration of your health condition), which renders you unable to instruct physicians regarding your care. If you do not have one, an Advanced Medical Directive form is available on my website (*www.moneylovelegacy.com*), though I always recommend you check with your attorney to insure the forms are complete and up-to-date in your state of residence. Changes in the law sometimes require additional updates to the legal forms.

Copy of Estate Plan.

The original is usually kept at the lawyer's office. You should have copies. The estate plan should including the following:

- A Revocable Living Trust or other trust arrangement
- Funding Instructions for the Trust
- Assignment of Personal Property

- Pour-over Will for husband
- Pour-over Will for wife
- Community Property Agreement
- Durable Power of Attorney for husband's property
- Durable Power of Attorney for wife's property
- Advance Health Care Directive with Living Will and *HIPAA Release for husband
- Advance Health Care Directive with Living Will and *HIPAA Release for wife

Authorization for release of health information

Insurance

Your binder should include information on all insurance policies: Life, Medical, Long-Term Care, Home Owner's, and Personal Property Insurance (if separate from the Homeowner's Policy). The information should include:

- The amount of coverage
- The issuing company
- Policy number
- Beneficiaries
- Agent's name and phone number
- Premium amount and due date (note: it's vital that insurance premiums are up to date and paid on time - if a payment is late, a policy may be cancelled)
- What does the policy pay for, and for how long?
- How long is the waiting period on the long-term care insurance?
- What conditions must be present before the long-term care policy can be activated?

Important Records and Documents

- Marriage license
- Birth certificates for parents and each child
- Title papers for house and other property
- Ownership papers for vehicles (registration, pink slip)
- Social security numbers
- Military discharge papers (veteran's funeral benefits may be available)
- Naturalization and citizenship documents (if applicable)
- Adoption records
- Contracts and leases (current and completed installment and maintenance)
- Combination to safe (if you store papers in a fireproof safe, keep the combination in a separate place that is easily accessible)
- Location of Safety Deposit Box, and location of access key
- Funeral instructions (See details below)
- Cancelled checks for at least three years (keep some cancelled checks and papers forever: house purchase; jewelry appraisal/ownership statements; brokerage statements, etc.)
- Tax records and returns for previous 5 years.
- Dividend and interest statements.
- Financial information
- Banking accounts
- Brokerage accounts
- Name and location of broker(s)
- Account numbers for each account
- Stocks or bonds held at locations outside brokerage house (safety deposit box, home safe, file cabinet, etc.)

- Retirement asset accounts (ie. IRA, Keogh)
- Other real estate information (amount of mortgages, equity to date, market value)
- Art (appraised value of antiques, coins, paintings, jewelry, etc.)
- IOUs – money owed to your family (all of these should be secured by a note)

Payment Amounts and Due Dates of:

- All mortgages (total loan, amount and due date, grace period and penalty for late payment)
- Taxes (income, property, business, land – anything for which you receive a tax bill)
- Outstanding loans (bank, car, boat, credit cards, Installment amount, due date)

Medical Records

- Names and phone number of doctors
- Birth dates (often medical records and insurance information are cataloged according to birth date. This can improve communication in an emergency or a crisis)
- List of allergies (vital if a family member is allergic to medication — penicillin, for example)
- Advance directives (this should be part of the estate plan which designates a durable power of attorney for medical decisions if a person is incapacitated)
- Major medical problems (this includes such conditions as diabetes or heart disease)
- List of medications, vitamins and herbal supplements
- Religious beliefs (this is particularly important in case blood transfusions are needed)

- Prior surgeries and major medical procedures (list past medical procedures including implanted medical devices such as pacemakers)
- Lifestyle information (alcohol or tobacco use)

Funeral Instructions

- Have you designated a funeral home?
- Is there a preference for burial or cremation?
- What does cost of funeral cover? (Most people who think they have a funeral policy have only purchased a plot)
- Do the plans involve transporting the body to another state? (Find out how: there are laws covering transportation of bodies across state lines.)
- Is there a preference to style of funeral service? (Some people prefer a traditional service; others want a postponed memorial service.)
- Is the obituary written? (This can be written now. It is much easier now than at the time of death.)

Appendix II

When Death Occurs

This checklist can prove very useful during an emergency. When my husband died, I couldn't function or think clearly. My daughters followed this list and found it extremely helpful in remaining calm and organized.

- A doctor or coroner must declare a person dead and sign a death certificate.
- Get at least 20 embossed copies of the original death certificate. You can get these from the hospital, the health department or the funeral director. (You will need an original copy of a death certificate for every agency or company you will have to deal with. Copies are not accepted by anyone).
- If a parent dies in a hospital or nursing home, the staff usually knows what to do next. Let them be your guide.

- If the death takes place at home, call or have someone else call the funeral home of your choice.
- Notify the lawyer, executor of the will and the insurance agent.
- Coordinate the supplying of food for the next few days.
- Decide on the time, place and kind of funeral service. (If you already have these in the binder, this part will be much easier).
- Make a list of family, friends, and colleagues to be informed. Decide who will inform them.
- Make lodging arrangements for out-of-town relatives and friends.
- Write obituary for appropriate newspapers. Know whom to ask for this.
- If flowers are not wanted, choose charity or hospital, etc. where gifts may be sent. Include this information in the obituary.
- Designate someone to pick up relatives who come in from out-of-town.
- Take extra home precautions against burglars, especially during funeral service. (Funeral arrangements are often published in local papers and burglars know no one is home).
- Designate a person to track flowers, gifts, and donations for later acknowledgement.

HELGA HAYSE is an author, professional speaker and seminar leader educating people on the role that money plays in family relationships. She speaks to financial and estate planning groups about how to help their clients overcome resistance to dealing with planning and legacy. Her personal experience with  transforming pain into regenerative legacy serves as a roadmap for parents and adult children to start the conversations that matter between generations.

Her previous book, *"Don't Worry about a Thing, Dear"- Why Women Need Financial Intimacy*, helps women understand why education about marital finances is vital for their protection if marriage ends.

Visit her Web sites :
www.moneylovelegacy.com
www.financialintimacy.com